W0006183

CARING FOR A LOVED ONE WITH MARY

A Seven Sorrows Prayer Companion

By Theresa Kiser

Our Sunday Visitor
Huntington, Indiana

Nihil Obstat
Msgr. Michael Heintz, Ph.D.
Censor Librorum

Imprimatur
Kevin C. Rhoades
Bishop of Fort Wayne-South Bend
October 19. 2022

The *Nihil Obstat* and *Imprimatur* are official declarations that a book is free from doctrinal or moral error. It is not implied that those who have granted the *Nihil Obstat* and *Imprimatur* agree with the contents, opinions, or statements expressed.

Scripture texts in this work are taken from the *New American Bible*, revised edition © 2010, 1991, 1986, 1970 Confraternity of Christian Doctrine, Washington, D.C. and are used by permission of the copyright owner. All Rights Reserved. No part of the New American Bible may be reproduced in any form without permission in writing from the copyright owner.

Every reasonable effort has been made to determine copyright holders of excerpted materials and to secure permissions as needed. If any copyrighted materials have been inadvertently used in this work without proper credit being given in one form or another, please notify Our Sunday Visitor in writing so that future printings of this work may be corrected accordingly.

Copyright © 2023 by Theresa Kiser
28 27 26 25 24 23   1 2 3 4 5 6 7 8 9

All rights reserved. With the exception of short excerpts for critical reviews, no part of this work may be reproduced or transmitted in any form or by any means whatsoever without permission from the publisher. For more information, visit: www.osv.com/permissions.

Our Sunday Visitor Publishing Division
Our Sunday Visitor, Inc.
200 Noll Plaza
Huntington, IN 46750
www.osv.com
1-800-348-2440

ISBN: 978-1-63966-008-7 (Inventory No. T2748)
1. RELIGION — Christian Theology — Mariology.
2. RELIGION — Christian Living — Devotional.
3. RELIGION — Christianity — Catholic.

eISBN: 978-1-63966-009-4
LCCN: 2022948988

Cover design and Interior design: Amanda Falk
Cover art: AdobeStock

PRINTED IN THE UNITED STATES OF AMERICA

To the sad, scared, sick, and lonely
— and to their caregivers.

To those who have shown me how to tend to loved ones
in need, and to Jesus through Our Lady of Sorrows.

Contents

Contents

Introduction

I didn't plan to become a caregiver; I doubt many people do. But when medical complications began to burden my infant son, I did the same thing you have done for your needy beloved one. We did the same thing the Blessed Mother did two thousand years ago. We said yes.

Caregiving is a difficult journey. It is born from love and grows love. It is practical, beautiful, needed, and meaningful. And yet — a lot of the time, it feels like absolute crap. (Our Lady might not phrase it that way, but I have a feeling she agrees!)

It's almost sacrilege in our Instagram culture to feel as badly (tired, worn out, emotional, frustrated, sad, etc.) for as long as caregivers do. Those of us who care for our ill or disabled children, parents, or other loved ones often have no idea how long we'll need to provide constant care. Yet we do, because of love.

As noble as it is, this love has very practical costs. It means long nights, laundry, cooking, cleaning, holding, comforting, reading, worrying, scheduling appointments, crying, driving, explaining, learning, filling out forms, and on and on and on. All of this takes a toll. It has to, because we're only human.

Sometimes the Lord asks us to commit to this kind of love over shorter periods of time, such as with a newborn, a child with a broken bone, or a family member recovering from surgery. The intensity and duration of the caregiving might vary, but Mary is there to meet us all the same.

The Seven Sorrows Found My Soul

It can only be grace that made me think of Mary in the first place. My son faced a difficult skin condition and other challenges, and the outlook for his quality of life was unknown. I was exhausted, scared, and sad — the complete opposite of the serene and happy image of motherhood that I'd seen advertised in paintings of the Madonna and Child.

Besides which, I couldn't help feeling that I *shouldn't* feel this way. No matter what happens, we are an "Easter people," right? I should be rejoicing, right?

I wasn't.

Call it a "whim"; call it "grace" (I do). For whatever reason, I started praying with the Seven Sorrows of Mary. I can't even remember how I stumbled across this old devotion, but as soon as I did, something changed in me.

No, I didn't instantly become a person who could go three weeks without sleep and never bat an eye. I still cried about *the things*. I still made myself do what needed to be done.

But I wasn't alone.

The Root of Sorrow Is Love

We're going to spend this book walking with Mary through her Seven Sorrows as she tended to the One who made himself needy, who allowed himself to suffer, and then to die, so that everything we're going through might be — and is! — worth something.

Before we do, since we'll spend so much time with Mary's sorrows (and our own), let me make one thing clear.

Caregiving for my son is one of the best things that has ever happened to me.

First, because I get to *be* with him. I get to see every minute of his day. I can almost hear the thoughts going through his mind because we get the luxury of time, even if it is very difficult time. Second, because I'm growing as a person. Third, because I've seen God work through my son's life and even through his struggles.

But mostly because of the first reason.

I love him.

I know that's why you're here too. Because you *love*.

I wish with all my heart that my son didn't have to bear such a weighty burden, that he could be healthy and carefree. I grieve for what I see him suffer.

But the line between grief and love is thin, if it even exists at all. Giving the care to my son that he needs offers me many (many!) opportunities each day to love him in the most practical way. It isn't just "showing" love, because most of what I do goes completely unnoticed. He may not "feel" loved by it, but he does feel food in his belly, medicine on schedule, clean clothes on his skin, and a cozy hug when he cries. It means that when he sleeps, I work. When he's awake, I tend to his needs. And when he's feeling really good, we get to play together.

My grief is deep. But so is my love, and my joy. My joy may appear muted by the tired bags under my eyes, but it's there. That love is the *reason*. It's also the product of caregiving. Every moment that I show up for him is a moment our love gets deeper. He can depend on me to love him, and I get the privilege of loving him.

Mary probably felt that too. She had the privilege of loving God as her Son — including all of the suffering that came with that privilege.

She knew, from the very start, that her Son would be different. She learned shortly thereafter that he would be killed. Like a diagnosis, Simeon's prophecy put Mary on the caregiver's track: one of being hyperaware of danger to the Beloved and of her own inadequacy to stop this external force.

But Mary didn't need to stop it; she did what she could, and when circumstances exceeded her abilities, she showed up. She stood by his side. She prayed. She grieved. She loved.

Am I a Caregiver?

Throughout this book, I'll use the term *caregiver*. It is easy to think that you don't "count" as a caregiver, so use this list as a guideline. For the purposes of this book, a caregiver is someone who provides emotional and/or practical support for a person who is hurting.

Often, that loved one will fall among the following: newborns, children, the elderly, ill, or disabled (including mental illnesses, physical illnesses, developmental delays, etc.), and anyone with other special needs.

Caregivers are not limited to family members, either. Throughout this book, I will be writing from my own perspective and experiences as a mother who is a long-term caregiver, but if you have embraced a profession that involves concern for the needs of others, you may deeply relate to Our Lady in this special way, too. These roles can range from nurses and hospice caregivers to nannies, social workers, and various volunteers.

Caregivers can relate in a special way to Mary's Seven Sorrows, and I attempt to draw out some of those meaningful connections in this book. However, I can't think of any person — caregiver or otherwise — whose soul wouldn't benefit from this incredible devotion to Our Lady!

This Road Is Blessed with Christ's Blood and Mary's Tears

Whatever event or gradual path has led to this point in your life, don't let circumstances rob you of awareness of this important truth: The root of caregiving is love. And love can only exist where God is. And Mary — who was literally full of God when she carried Jesus in her womb, and to whom the angel said "the Lord is with you" — was asked to suffer in this way as well.

We are not put on this path as punishment, or as a rejection from the "perfect" life. Rather, through caregiving, we may be blessed with a rare opportunity: to love Christ (by loving our own needy beloved) as Mary loved him; to feel for another what Mary felt for Jesus; and in this way, to approach the life that Jesus asks of all of us — to carry our crosses and to follow him through suffering and death into eternal life.

We are not "off course." This is no detour. We are exactly where we are meant to be.

God in his goodness has given us two sets of footprints to follow: Christ's and his Blessed Mother's, whose steps followed her Son's as nearly as you follow your needy beloved when they wander close to their limits. Since Mary has walked this road before us, she can gently catch our arm and steady us when we wander close to limits of our own.

By praying the Seven Sorrows of Mary, we can meet her there, on the road to Calvary, and here, in the living room, kitchen, and at our beloved's bedside.

Heaven has charted this road. Day by day, night by night, we walk it. And we are not alone.

How to Pray the Seven Sorrows

Devotion to Our Lady of Sorrows began with Christ himself. Jesus told St. John the Evangelist, at the foot of the cross, "Behold, your mother" (Jn 19:27). Many hundreds of years later, in 1239, Mary herself appeared to seven men in Florence, Italy, asking them to meditate on her sorrows. They obeyed, founding the order of the Servites (the Servants of Mary), and they began to spread devotion to her *dolors*. Seven hundred years later, Our Lady of Sorrows appeared at Fatima during her final apparition there in 1917. Finally, in the 1980s, the Blessed Mother appeared to schoolchildren in Kibeho, Rwanda, urging them, among other messages of love, to pray the Rosary of the Seven Sorrows.

Meditating on Our Lady's Seven Sorrows honors Mary's suffering, consoles her maternal wounds, expresses gratitude for her pivotal role in our salvation, and allows for a deeper relationship with Christ's passion through Mary.

Moreover, praying in this way is doable. Even for we who are time-strapped, worn-out, caregivers.

Here's how to participate in this devotion: Pray seven Hail Marys, meditating on one of Mary's sorrows during each prayer. It looks like this:

First Hail Mary — The Prophecy of Simeon
Second Hail Mary — The Flight into Egypt
Third Hail Mary — The Loss of the
    Child Jesus in the Temple of Jerusalem

Fourth Hail Mary — The Meeting of Mary with
   Jesus on His Way to Calvary
Fifth Hail Mary — The Death of Jesus
Sixth Hail Mary — The Piercing of the Side of Jesus
   and His Descent from the Cross
Seventh Hail Mary — The Burial of the Body of Jesus

There is no required reading to be done at any part of the meditation. These are stories we all know (and will gain even more familiarity with throughout this book). It's as simple as seven Hail Marys and as profound as God's grace allows.

There is also a longer Seven Sorrows of Mary Chaplet (which is explained in the appendix). With the chaplet, you spend a little more time with each sorrow during prayer time. However, I'm writing to caregivers, so I'm going to keep it simple and focus on the seven Hail Marys. You can always expand your prayer routine later if you like.

THE HAIL MARY
Hail Mary, Full of grace, the Lord is with you. Blessed are you among women, and blessed is the fruit of your womb, Jesus. Holy Mary, Mother of God, pray for us sinners, now and at the hour of our death. Amen.

Let's take a look at some of the benefits and advantages of praying the Seven Sorrows, and why it's a wonderful prayer for everyone, but especially for caregivers.

Benefits of Praying the Seven Sorrows

It's quick. Time is hard to come by these days, especially for caregivers. This rich prayer is surprisingly quick. With fewer total Hail Marys than a single decade of the Rosary, praying the Seven Sorrows can take as little as four minutes.

It's easy to remember. The Hail Mary is well known and is easy to learn. You can keep the Seven Sorrows printed on a sheet of paper until you have them memorized, which doesn't take long, since they follow the story of the Gospel in an easy-to-remember way.

You don't need to hold anything. No need to hold a rosary for this devotion. No Bible or meditation booklet is required. The Seven Sorrows of Mary devotion is hands-free (which can be useful when you're holding your needy beloved in the middle of the night, or praying amidst the "pots and pans" during the day).

> *Know that even when you are in the kitchen, Our Lord moves amidst the pots and pans.*
> — *St. Teresa of Ávila,*
> **The Book of the Foundations**

It's easy to keep track of which Hail Mary you're on. Since each Hail Mary corresponds to a different moment in Mary's and Jesus' lives, you won't lose track of where you are in the devotion. If you get distracted, simply consider which story you were just meditating on, and you'll know where to start up again.

It's scriptural. There is so much richness in praying with Scripture, but when you are tending to someone suffering, it can seem difficult to keep regular habits that require use of an item (such as a Bible), since your schedule can be disturbed and re-written from day-to-day-to-day. Yet the Seven Sorrows of Mary devotion allows us to pray deeply with the stories of Scripture — from memory — and to meet Christ and his Blessed Mother there. It is a true blessing.

It meets you where you are. As a caregiver, sometimes the energy to do much of anything beyond caregiving simply isn't there. With this devotion, we show up to Our Lady of Sorrows as we are, and she — the Mediatrix of all grace — pours her love (and her Son's love!) on us. On days when we pray the devotion without much depth, she is there suffering with us. On other days, we may pray more deeply, and God's grace is there to meet us deeply, to find us in the midst of our sufferings, fill us with his grace, and pull us closer and closer to him through his Blessed Mother.

BENEFITS SUMMARY

Praying the Seven Sorrows is quick, easy to remember, you don't have to hold anything, it's easy to keep track of which Hail Mary you are on, it's scriptural, it meets you where you are, and heaven has promised us spiritual rewards.

Heaven has promised us spiritual rewards. In addition to all the immediate and practical benefits above (which are encouragement enough to pray the Seven Sorrows!), in various private revelations, Mary and Jesus have made several promises to those who pray this devotion. They didn't hold back. Let's take a look.

Promises and Graces for Those Devoted to the Seven Sorrows

Our Blessed Mother revealed seven promises to St. Bridget of Sweden in the early fourteenth century. These promises, Mary said, will be granted to those who honor her daily by saying seven Hail Marys while meditating on her sorrows. The promises are:

1. "I will grant peace to their families."
2. "They will be enlightened about the divine Mysteries."

3. "I will console them in their pains, and I will accompany them in their work."

4. "I will give them as much as they ask for as long as it does not oppose the adorable will of my divine Son or the sanctification of their souls."

5. "I will defend them in their spiritual battles with the infernal enemy, and I will protect them at every instant of their lives."

6. "I will visibly help them at the moments of their deaths — they will see the face of their mother."

7. "I have obtained this grace from my divine Son, that those who propagate this devotion to my tears and dolors will be taken directly from this earthly life to eternal happiness, since all their sins will be forgiven, and my Son and I will be their eternal consolation and joy."

In addition to these promises, St. Alphonsus Liguori, in his book *The Glories of Mary*, records four graces which Jesus promised to give those devoted to his Mother's Seven Sorrows:

1. That those who before death invoke the divine Mother in the name of her sorrows should obtain true re-

pentance of all their sins.

2. That he would protect all who have this devotion in their tribulations, and that he would protect them especially at the hours of their deaths.

3. That he would impress upon their minds the remembrance of his passion, and that they should have their reward for it in heaven.

4. That he would commit such devout clients to the hands of Mary, with the power to dispose of them in whatever manner she might please, and to obtain for them all the graces she might desire.

With all these promises and graces, the ones that jump out to me most as a caregiver are promises one, three, and four. Just knowing that Mary has promised to work at my side, that she wills to give me as much as I ask for (which, mainly, is help for my needy beloved!), and finally that she will grant peace to my family — these are my most immediate desires. To have discovered that Our Lady promised these things, frankly, gives me hope.

The Lies That Degrade Our Sorrow

There are so many reasons why people don't pray the Seven Sorrows of Mary. Besides not really knowing about this beautiful tradition, it is easy to get snared by the cultural lies which tell us to avoid difficulty and suffering. Jesus' teachings were confusing (and countercultural) when he told his followers, "If anyone wishes to come after me, he must deny himself and take up his cross daily and follow me" (Lk 9:23).

With the Seven Sorrows of Mary, we meditate on Mary's "cross" of love for her Son through seven distinct sorrowful events during her life. It is a moving prayer, yet the concept clashes with several lies that we may be conditioned to believe. Let's look at some of these lies and discover the truth about how the Seven Sorrows of Mary can help us carry our cross of love for our needy beloved.

How many of these lies have tempted you?

My sorrow is shameful. In our Instagram culture, anything less than "perfect" is fair game for derision. We are told to buck up, put on a good attitude, and download a meditation app. We are expected to be able to handle life easily, no matter what challenges come our way.

It can be hard to admit — even to ourselves — that we are struggling. That our sorrow is deep. Yet this cultural shame we have around sorrow is an absolute lie.

Sorrow is not shameful. It is the flip side of love. Show me a life without sorrow, and I'll show you a life without love. Sorrow is part of being human, part of living a full life. We do not need to fear it.

Furthermore, God knows we will experience sorrow in this fallen world. He does not expect us to avoid it.

If we think that holy people do not have sorrow because they have faith, let Mary bust that myth for us. She is the holiest among women, and she experienced greater sorrow than any of us.

Sorrow is not shameful; sorrow is part of a fully human life.

I'm alone in this. Again with social media. Please. If you've ever scrolled through a feed, you've seen the smiling, healthy, seemingly carefree faces. It can make us feel that we are alone. Even in person, many people do not discuss their sorrows (see Lie #1), so it can be a challenge to find others who understand. But the fact is, others who sorrow do exist.

Once I embraced the identity of "caregiver" on top of parent, I had a conversation with a caregiver who was taking care of an elderly man in outpatient hospice. My soul soared after that conversation! After having had lots of talks with fellow parents, in which I felt like we were just in very different circumstances, I finally found someone (not a parent!) who *got it*. He understood the night wakings, the chronic sleep deprivation, the appointments, the thousands of little details that suddenly take over. We laughed about the same things. It caught me totally by surprise. That conversation was a true gift!

My heart soared the same way when I found the Seven Sorrows of Mary. Not only can some people on earth understand, but also the saints and angels in heaven. We are NOT alone. When we walk the Seven Sorrows with Mary, we grow deeper and deeper in this freeing truth.

I'm doing something wrong. We think "it isn't supposed to be this way" because we are *made for heaven*. We know deep down how life is supposed to be (and will be!) in heaven. Our struggle as humans is that we're not there yet.

And this truth doesn't need to exacerbate the suffering; instead, it can lift the stress of the lie. And it *is* stressful. How many times have you shared a struggle with someone only to have them try to argue you out of your pain? Things like, "Well if you look at it this way, then it really isn't so bad," or "If only you had *this* mindset," or "If only you practiced better self-care."

Such statements, while well intentioned, often fail to address the true need. Our task is not to avoid sorrow; in fact, we may be unable to.

Instead, our task is to walk through the sorrow, knowing that it is temporary (however long temporary may be) and that God will give it value. Sometimes a change of mindset can help, but changing my mindset doesn't take away my needy beloved's cross. He will continue to suffer, and I will continue to suffer with him through love. I pray that God will "take away this cup," but only if it is his will (and if it is his will, as soon as possible, please!).

No one cares or understands. This lie goes right along with Lie #2. It is not wrong to feel that no one cares. Perhaps you have shared your sorrows, and the reaction has been all wrong. Perhaps you feel you have no one to tell. I've been there. I promise you.

I felt this way for a long time before I finally found a helpful combination of self-validation, understanding of my own feelings, reaching out to people I hadn't before, and asking for what I needed in a more direct way. Oh yeah, and grace.

There are people in my life who haven't experienced what I have, yet they understand as much as they can through empathy. It took me a while to find them, but they exist. Since then, I've discovered additional contacts and support groups, which can be invaluable aids in bringing connection within an isolating culture.

Furthermore, God cares: "Even the hairs of your head have

all been counted" (Lk 12:7). He loved you into being. He cares about you, your grief, and your joy. Mary's Seven Sorrows give evidence of this care. Jesus gave Mary the consolation of John (and all of us) from the cross. Perhaps, in turn, he gives us his Mother as we carry our crosses, and as we help our needy beloveds to carry theirs.

Meditating on death or sorrows will make me a Debbie Downer. There is an old Latin phrase, *Memento mori*, which means, "Remember death." Meditating on death and our own limitations can be an important step in growing in maturity, especially when that meditation is done within the context of the hope that our faith gives us.

In spite of this, "remembering death" and contemplating sorrows is a countercultural act. People may be caught off guard if you express a devotion to Our Lady of Sorrows, or if you spend time every day meditating on her *dolors*. But we are fortunate in that we know Mary's sorrows are only one part of the picture; the destiny of her Seven Sorrows is her Seven Joys; the destiny of the crucifixion is the Resurrection; and the destiny of our own sufferings here in this "vale of tears" is heaven, with all its joys.

Meditating on the Seven Sorrows will not make you a Debbie Downer. Rather, it creates an opportunity to delve deeper into a

---

MARY'S SEVEN SORROWS BEAR FRUIT IN HER SEVEN JOYS

1) The Annunciation
2) The Visitation
3) The Birth of Our Lord
4) The Adoration of Jesus by the Magi
5) The Finding of the Child Jesus in the Temple
6) The Resurrection of Our Lord
7) The Assumption of Mary in Body and Soul into Heaven

---

relationship with him who died for us, who gave us his mother, and who rose, that we may rise as well.

This period of my life is ruined/ wasted. It is a great comfort to know the truth that shuts down Lie #6. The truth is: Nothing is wasted that is offered to God.

God can make use of every little sacrifice and struggle that we make or undergo in caregiving, and of every ache, pain, discomfort, and suffering of our needy beloved. Although this doesn't take away the struggle, it offers something important: the knowledge that every moment of these wearying (sometimes grueling) days is used.

When we offer to God our struggle (and that of our loved one), he will use every single ounce for a greater purpose than we can imagine. He turns our meager offerings (even when that offering is just enduring through the day) into unfathomable riches. Maybe we will glimpse the fruits of our work while we are still alive, but maybe instead we'll only see the full impact of our lives from heaven.

Either way, the truth remains. Nothing is wasted.

It will always be like this. Sometimes it really feels like it will be this way forever. Only God knows how long your loved one will be needy. Only God knows his plan for your caregiving. Who can say but him?

What we do know is that all things, even wonderful things, eventually come to an end. Difficult times end too.

This is a season. Just as cold winter warms and blooms into spring, so too will caregiving eventually lead to a new season for you and your loved one.

> *The smallest thing, when done for the love of God, is priceless.*
> *— St. Teresa of Ávila,*
> **The Book of the Foundations**

In the meantime, when it's difficult to keep going on what may be a long journey, remember that you are not alone. Mary is here to walk through your sorrows with you, as you walk alongside her.

No one can walk this difficult path for your needy beloved, but when you walk by his or her side, you are not alone either.

Mary and all of heaven are with you. When you pray the Seven Sorrows of Mary, you'll know it.

Praying this rich tradition of our faith has yielded so much fruit in my life, and Our Lady's promises show that there is more fruit to come. This prayer certainly doesn't take away our sorrows, or even lessen them, but Mary's example combats so many of those lies that slither through our culture and threaten to snare us in bitterness, doubt, and despair. Crushing the serpent under her feet, Mary shows us instead the light of truth.

There is an appointed time for everything, and a time for every affair under the heavens. A time to give birth, and a time to die; a time to plant, and a time to uproot the plant. A time to kill, and a time to heal; a time to tear down, and a time to build. A time to weep, and a time to laugh; a time to mourn, and a time to dance. A time to scatter stones, and a time to gather them; a time to embrace, and a time to be far from embraces. A time to seek, and a time to lose; a time to keep, and a time to cast away. A time to rend, and a time to sew; a time to be silent, and a time to speak. A time to love, and a time to hate; a time of war, and a time of peace.
— Ecclesiastes 3:1–8

We need this light, especially since these cultural lies not only keep us from prayer but also erode and degrade the work that we are called to do in this difficult phase of our lives. When we meditate on her sorrows, Mary reveals her Son to us, and we may even catch a glimpse of where he is working in our day-to-day lives.

Where Do We Go from Here?

Throughout this book, we'll explore the Seven Sorrows of Mary and reflect on how they correspond to the experience of caregiving. Noticing the parallels between my life and Mary's has softened my heart to these meditations, given me instant consolation, and — over time — has deepened my relationship with Jesus through his Blessed Mother.

This book does not attempt to replace some of the rich books that go deep into Mary's Seven Sorrows; rather, this is a starting point, a meeting place between today's caregiver and Our Lady of Sorrows. Where you take it from here is up to you!

I used to think that a holy person would be ever cheerful and serene. But Mary showed me otherwise. Her close relationship with God gave her more peace than anyone else, but that peace *included* a great deal of suffering. Mary's holiness did not shield her from situations that could inspire loneliness, frustration, fear, or grief. Instead, those difficult experiences are so intertwined with her holiness that it is a disservice to forget them.

In this way, her sorrows remind me that my own sufferings are part of God's loving plan. When I try (unsuccessfully, I might add) to avoid the difficulties of my circumstances, I may be closing myself off to the grace he generously offers me within them. When I struggle to find the strength, I am comforted to know — at the very least — that Mary walked this road before me. There is no reason why she would abandon me when she knows so deeply how my heart aches.

Your path of caregiving will reveal its own sorrows particular to you, particular to the saint God made you to be. He is leading you through the steps by which you will most intimately relate to his Son, by means of his Blessed Mother, if you allow it.

Join me in walking through these Seven Sorrows of Mary. She will share our tears as we share in hers. She will show you that you are not alone; that God has not abandoned you to the evils of this world; and that, as with her life, God will use *your* life to lead you to him and others to love.

Chapter One
The Prophecy of Simeon
FEAR

The first Sorrow of Mary is the Prophecy of Simeon, described in the Gospel of Luke 2:25–38:

Now there was a man in Jerusalem whose name was Simeon. This man was righteous and devout, awaiting the consolation of Israel, and the holy Spirit was upon him. It had been revealed to him by the holy Spirit that he should not see death before he had seen the Messiah of the Lord. He came in the Spirit into the temple; and when the parents brought in the child Jesus to perform the custom of the law in regard to him, he took him into his arms and blessed God, saying:

> "Now, Master, you may let your servant go
> in peace, according to your word,
> for my eyes have seen your salvation,
> which you prepared in sight of all the peoples,
> a light for revelation to the Gentiles,
> and glory for your people Israel."

The child's father and mother were amazed at what was said about him; and Simeon blessed them and said to Mary his mother, "Behold, this child is destined for the fall and rise of many in Israel, and to be a sign that will be contradicted (and you yourself a sword will pierce) so that the thoughts of many hearts may be revealed."

There was also a prophetess, Anna, the daughter of Phanuel, of the tribe of Asher. She was advanced in years, having lived seven years with her husband after her marriage, and then as a widow until she was eighty-four. She never left the temple, but worshiped night and day with fasting and prayer. And coming forward at that very time, she gave thanks to God and spoke about the child to all who were awaiting the redemption of Jerusalem.

The Diagnosis Changes Everything

The day of Jesus' presentation in the temple was supposed to be a joyful day. In some ways, it was! When Mary presented the baby Jesus in the temple, it was so wonderful that it numbers among her Seven Joys. Yet mere minutes later, she receives the devastating news.

"All my joy was changed into sorrow at that moment," Our Lady later said to Saint Matilda. Simeon had foretold a terrible truth: Jesus was "a sign that will be contradicted."

For some people it's a moment: one elderly fall, one earth-shattering conversation with a doctor, one terrible accident. For others, like me, it's a series of moments. None of them were very dramatic. But all demonstrated that our family had a medical mountain to climb. I could not deny that fact, and nothing was as it had been before.

The Virgin Mary, I suppose, belonged to the former group. With Simeon's prophecy, everything changed.

Our Lady "kept all these things, reflecting on them in her

heart" (Lk 2:19). She knew — by Simeon's prophecy — that whatever "a sign that will be contradicted" meant also entailed the salvation of the world. What price did this mean for her Son? That's something she found out gradually.

Our Lady revealed to Saint Teresa that she learned the things Jesus would suffer little by little. When we walk through the Bible, we can see the signs as well: People undervalued Jesus ("Is he not the carpenter's son?" [Mt 13:55]); they considered him a blasphemer, a madman, or a drunkard; they considered him a nuisance, a threat to their power; they hunted him down to kill him; they conspired against him; his friends betrayed him; and on and on, down to the very last lashing of the whip.

When someone puts our loved one's path of suffering into words (as Simeon's prophecy did), it both clarifies and destroys. Like Mary, we carry a burden of sorrow within us.

In many cases, that sorrow deepens with every new loss or every moment of drawn-out suffering. Originally, we may not have understood exactly what the diagnosis meant for our lives and for the life of our needy beloved, but as we accompany them, we find out. The cup is bitter. The sorrow is great.

> *My life is worn out by sorrow.*
> — Psalm 31:11

Let This Cup Pass

Later in his life, Jesus would approach another "diagnosis" when Pontius Pilate condemned him to death by crucifixion. Jesus had an idea of what awaited him after he prayed in the Garden of Gethsemane. He prayed so hard that the Father would "let this cup pass" from him that he sweated blood.

Did Mary, I wonder, beg God in that same way after Simeon's prophecy? Did she weep for the perfect baby in her arms and beg that God would find some other way to save the world, echoing, as Jesus did, "Not my will, but yours be done"? Perhaps she prayed while holding her needy Beloved. Perhaps he heard her. Perhaps, all those years later, he prayed with his Mother's very words.

"My Father, if it is possible, let this cup pass from me; yet, not as I will, but as you will" (Mt 26:39). It is a difficult prayer to pray. The second part anyway.

Recently, anxiously, awaiting test results, I called another caregiver, a mom who I knew would understand. She had suffered before in this "waiting place." She had gone through cancer herself and had received several diagnoses for her children.

She told me how angry she got with God. She laid all her fear in front of him in prayer.

When she had cancer and awaited the results to see if the

treatment had induced a fatal leukemia, she told God, "I don't want to die!" His answer in response was a question: "What if your death is the thing that causes a conversion in heart for your children? What if that is the thing that saves them?"

It helped her to remember that if the diagnosis is the difference between salvation and hell, then suffering is worth it. "If your hand or foot causes you to sin, cut it off and throw it away. It is better for you to enter into life maimed or crippled than with two hands or two feet to be thrown into eternal fire. And if your eye causes you to sin, tear it out and throw it away. It is better for you to enter into life with one eye than with two eyes to be thrown into fiery Gehenna" (Mt 18:8–9).

It's not an easy thought.

It's not an easy road.

Mary knows this. She has felt the destructive power of a diagnosis. She watched her innocent Son "decline" as more and more sinful people doubted and conspired against him year by year.

The carefree "before" is altered, replaced by a sorrowful "after."

"Whenever I saw his hands and feet, I was absorbed in fresh grief, thinking of how he would be crucified," Mary told Saint Bridget. Grief stayed with her, hour by hour, as long as she lived.

And here, in our grief, Mary meets us.

Anger

"It should not be this way!" How many times must Mary have exclaimed those words (even if just in private prayer). Indeed, it should not. Jesus — of all people — did not deserve to suffer. He deserved glory. He deserved recognition, praise, attention, and worship. He deserved the glories of Easter, and yet humanity handed him death.

It was not fair. It was not just.

Our loved ones do not deserve their sufferings either. It is not fair. Because we love them, we know what they deserve: more love! Greater love than we can give! Indeed, because of Christ, they should inherit the glories of Easter too! And yet, life hands them suffering.

Mary's beloved Son suffered to bring about a greater joy than humanity has known: heaven. In order for us to share in it, he said, "Whoever wishes to come after me must

Just take everything exactly as it is, put it in God's hands and leave it with Him. Then you will be able to rest in Him — really rest — and start the next day, as a new life.
— St. Teresa Benedicta of the Cross, **Paths to Interior Silence**

deny himself, take up his cross, and follow me" (Mt 16:24). Mary surely carried her cross. We carry ours. Our needy beloveds carry theirs.

These crosses are not punishments but are the very means to our salvation. If Jesus was given the treatment he deserved on earth, then we would be worse off, because heaven would be closed off to us. If we and our needy beloveds had been dealt a different "hand of cards" in this life, then our souls might be worse off. Otherwise, I can't believe that God would allow it.

He loves us. He loves his Mother. None of this is done as torture. It is done as the means to bring us to that joy and wholeness for which we have so longed, joy which we will find in heaven by the grace of God.

Mary knows it is not fair. She also knows that when we can't change things, the only choice is to go through it. And going through it is worth it.

Conclusion

Simeon's prophecy changed everything for Mary. A diagnosis, or suspected diagnosis, can change everything for us, too. In some ways, we may understand Mary better than those who haven't experienced such devastating news. We share in her anger. We know the injustice. We beg and beg that this cup might pass.

The more we meditate on this first Sorrow of Mary, the more our sorrow and our anger can unite with hers. We know too well that sometimes we cannot stop the track our needy beloveds are on; we cannot take their pain away. But we stay with them in love, day by day, as Mary did.

Pray, hope, and don't worry. Worry is useless. God is merciful and will hear your prayer.
— Motto attributed to Padre Pio

As Christ's death approached, "the sword" which pierced Mary's soul penetrated deeper and deeper. "That sword of sorrow approached every hour as the Passion grew near," St. Alphonsus Liguori writes in *The Glories of Mary*. Your needy beloved may be on a track to either improve, remain steady, or decline in condition over time. When you feel the deep sorrow of anticipation and loss, or see the picture of your needy beloved's suffering growing painfully more clear, call on Mary. She weeps with you. She *knows*.

∼ *PRAYER* ∼

*Our Lady of Sorrows, when Simeon prophesied that Jesus would
be contradicted, and that a sword would pierce your soul, a sorrow
met you and remained with you always. I am devastated to watch
my needy beloved suffer this way. The thought of his (her) current
and future sufferings is more than I can bear. Please beg God on
my behalf to take away this cup of suffering if at all possible. But
— as you and your Son did — I insist that not my will be done, but
God's, because salvation for me and my needy beloved is my greatest
desire. The Lord can do all things. Beg him to have mercy. Beg him
to make use of any suffering he asks us to endure. Our Lady, do not
abandon me in my grief but accompany me, as I accompany you in
the meditation on your Seven Sorrows. Bring my petitions to God
and lead me closer to your Son as I tend to my needy beloved. Amen.*

Chapter Two
The Flight into Egypt
ISOLATION

The second Sorrow of Mary is the flight into Egypt, described in the Gospel of Matthew 2:13–18:

> When they had departed, behold, the angel of the Lord appeared to Joseph in a dream and said, "Rise, take the child and his mother, flee to Egypt, and stay there until I tell you. Herod is going to search for the child to destroy him." Joseph rose and took the child and his mother by

night and departed for Egypt. He stayed there until the death of Herod, that what the Lord had said through the prophet might be fulfilled, "Out of Egypt I called my son."

When Herod realized that he had been deceived by the magi, he became furious. He ordered the massacre of all the boys in Bethlehem and its vicinity two years old and under, in accordance with the time he had ascertained from the magi. Then was fulfilled what had been said through Jeremiah the prophet:

> "A voice was heard in Ramah,
> sobbing and loud lamentation;
> Rachel weeping for her children,
> and she would not be consoled,
> since they were no more."

Fear

As a caregiver, you know that sometimes the situation overtakes us. Sometimes it is too great a sorrow to bear. In those moments, the heart can yearn to flee to some carefree location where love doesn't hurt so badly. In Mary's case, she literally fled, with the child Jesus in her arms and Saint Joseph at her side. But Mary knows — as do we — that distance cannot take away the fear that comes from loving one who suffers.

The world tempts us with many reasons to fear: fear that our needy beloved will never recover; fear that they will die; fear that we will not be able to help them; fear that they will continue to suffer; fear that they will lose hope; fear that *we* will lose hope …

Mary shared many of these fears.

In her case, a powerful man wanted to kill her son. He had the means to do it, too.

Sometimes disease or mental illness has the means to overtake our loved one. This awareness brings us very close to Our Lady in the flight into Egypt, traveling from cave to cave. In the same way, as we make our way from day to day in the hope of eluding the powerful forces that threaten our needy beloved, Mary remains at our side. She knows what it's like.

Scripture tells us again and again, "Do not be afraid."

Our Lady, in response, says her fiat: "May it be done to me according to your word" (Lk 1:38).

But let us not think for a moment that trusting in God's plan necessarily means perfect ease in the face of anguish. We can hear Mary's anguish — in her third sorrow, the loss of the child Jesus in the temple, which we will reflect on in depth in the next chapter — in the first words she says to her Son when she finally finds him in Jerusalem, "Son, why have you done this to us?" (Lk

2:48) She trusted God, but she also felt the sorrow which that trust sometimes entails.

Jesus felt this anguish so fully in the Garden of Gethsemane that he sweat blood, begging his Father, "Let this cup pass from me; yet, not as I will, but as you will" (Mt 26:39).

Faith Is a Gift from God

When caring for a loved one wears down the mind, body, and soul, we can be tempted to imagine that if we only trusted God enough, we would not be afraid. Such thoughts are possible snares that drag us down during the good and beautiful (and draining) work of loving another.

The truth is, faith is a gift from God. Sometimes he gives us moments (or longer!) of a trust that is so strong that we cannot fear. In those moments of grace, we can see all things through his eyes and understand that the immense suffering of earth is nothing compared to the glories which that suffering gains if offered to God. These moments of trust can be hard to come by. St. Thérèse of Lisieux describes these moments of the spiritual journey as times when Jesus "hides" from us for the sake of our souls' progress. During these times, for us caregivers, God offers us a special gift: Our Lady of Sorrows to accompany us.

Mary fled the powers which threatened to harm her needy

Beloved. In our way, we do too. We may not know exactly what fate awaits the ones we love; neither did Our Lady. And herein lies our solace.

Jesus may hide himself, but we know he is there.
— *St. Thérèse of Lisieux,* **The Story of a Soul**

Far from Home

Many who have never been a caregiver will not understand. It can be hard to connect with peers when your and their daily concerns seem otherworldly to each other, with theirs so far removed from the context of your day-to-day caregiving. More to the point, it can be hard to connect with peers when you never get a chance to spend time with peers.

In this way, we get a chance to relate to Mary during her second sorrow. In Egypt, she was separated from her relatives and culture. She was apart from those who might understand. She couldn't spend time with them. Those with whom Mary could spend time were not familiar. They were Egyptians, and Mary did not speak the language.

When we encounter others who don't know what it's like to tend to a needy beloved, or — more poignantly — who don't know the struggles particular to tending to *our* needy beloved, it can feel as though we are speaking two different languages. Furthermore, the "culture" of our lives when we are caregiving (our priorities and values, in addition to language) is very different than the non-caregiving culture. Different sacrifices are demanded. Different joys are cherished.

Even if we haven't traveled to a foreign country to tend to our needy beloved, we still don't necessarily feel "at home." For some, caregiving *does* entail a move out of one's home, city, or state. For others, the ailment "moves in" and creates its own shift. Either way, the routines we once knew are disrupted as we take on the work of caring for someone we love so much, who needs so much.

Unknown Duration

When Joseph told Mary about his dream, Mary had to trust her husband, take her Son, and go. The family ventured together away from the land of their births into Egypt, a country which carried the sting of hundreds of years of slavery for their ancestors. Sometimes when we're called to give care to a needy beloved, we sense the sting of sorrow in advance; we know it will be difficult.

Furthermore, like Mary and Joseph, we often have no idea how long the difficulty will last. A loved one in hospice may be waiting for death, and we know neither the day nor the hour (see Mt 24:36). Another ill loved one may be hoping for recovery, which is a road of hope that must often be deferred as the winding healing journey makes its advances and recessions. Another loved one may have a long life ahead with challenges all the way.

Each of these situations contains its own joys, graces, and sorrows. We tend to our needy beloved because we love, and that love itself is a gift from God. To deny that love for our needy beloved would be to deny our very selves.

Still, the unknown duration of our caregiving presents a struggle. It is very difficult to continue day after day, night after night, without

The road is narrow. He who wishes to travel it more easily, must cast off all things and use the cross as his cane. In other words, he must be truly resolved to suffer willingly, for the love of God, in all things.
— St. John of the Cross, **The Ascent of Mount Carmel**

reprieve, not knowing when a break might come (and perhaps, dreading the day that it does, for what it might mean for the needy beloved).

Mary experienced this; the flight into Egypt lasted years. And even such an unknown duration brings potential for spiritual growth. When the duration of a suffering is unknown, making our peace dependent on external factors fails us. We have an opportunity instead to build the house of our souls on rock, not sand, with the grace of Jesus through Mary.

Isolated but Not Alone

Even as they journeyed far from home, in fear, for an unknown amount of time, God gave Mary a grace: He gave her Joseph. Joseph, as we know, was not as close to Jesus as Mary was. After all, Joseph sinned (unlike Mary), and he hadn't been part of Jesus' conception. All this is to say, if Mary were to have an "equal" to share her sorrow, Joseph wasn't it.

Nevertheless, Joseph was the one God chose.

When Mary struggled to bear the weight of fear for her Son, Joseph shared it too. When Mary felt awkward in an unknown land, Joseph felt it too.

God doesn't abandon us to face these struggles. He gives us *someone*. And, like Joseph, he *makes* that person up to the task. He provides the necessary grace. Joseph, for all his imperfection, was the *perfect* person for Mary during that time — and for Jesus.

Perhaps a person sharing your sorrow is your spouse, just as it was for Mary. Or, perhaps your spouse did not stay for the struggle, or is grieving on a different timeline or in a different manner than you. Also possible is that the person whom God put in your life to accompany you is a sibling, parent, or friend. It's not unlike God to work through multiple people, even strangers, in surprising and little ways.

This person will disappoint you; they will not be able to take your sorrow away, as Joseph couldn't take away Mary's sorrow. Sometimes the person who accompanies you will also need you to accompany and comfort them, as I'm sure Mary did for Joseph.

The point is, as isolated as you may feel, you are not alone — not really.

And if you can't think of anyone who can offer you solace from time to time on this earth, remember that heavenly help is here, through Our Lady. She will "fill in the gaps" when others fall short and when the burden gets too heavy.

And there's one more Person who comforted Our Lady in Egypt, someone who loves you too. I think you can guess who I'm thinking of.

OK, I'll come out and say it: Jesus!

Conclusion

In all these regards, we walk in the footsteps of Our Lady, the refugee and foreigner, the woman willing to venture far from home to protect the One she loved. As we venture far from home to do right by our needy beloved, we can remember that in our venturing, Mary is with us.

Even when others don't speak "our language," Mary does. She

knows our struggles — and those of our needy beloved — intimately, and as we join our sorrows to hers, she pours grace back into the rugged terrain of our journey.

Mary has fled with me to this unknown land of my loved one's needs and holds within her palms a powerful promise: All will be used for good. This suffering is not the end. Not for me, and not for my needy beloved.

God's plans are as unknown and lovely to me as the sunflower is to the seed, as the Resurrection was to the Holy Family during their time as refugees in Egypt. All this love is more "worth it" than we can pretend to understand.

And if that means being unknown for an unknowable amount of time in an unknown land with a threatened future, then Mary teaches us: So be it, *fiat*.

May the Child Jesus be your guiding star in the desert of this present life.
— *Padre Pio,*
Correspondence with His Spiritual Directors

∼ *PRAYER* ∼

Our Lady of Sorrows, I wish that I could take my needy beloved and run far away from his (her) suffering, as you ran with Jesus away from King Herod. This vale of tears feels to me like a foreign land, devoid of the comforts and securities that I used to rely upon. My only security is in the endless mercy of your Son, Jesus. Please ask him to grace me with the strength to love as you did, just as Jesus graced you with his smiles and snuggles along your fearful journey. When I feel alone, please pour God's grace into my soul. Let me remember this sorrow of yours, and grant me confidence in your love for me and for my needy beloved. Pray for me. Stand by my side. Comfort my needy beloved. We follow in your blessed steps and present all our fear and isolation at your feet. Make use of these sorrows as God made use of yours. Amen.

Chapter Three

The Loss of the Child Jesus in the Temple of Jerusalem

SELF-DOUBT

The third Sorrow of Mary is the loss of the child Jesus in the temple, described in the Gospel of Luke 2:41–52:

Each year his parents went to Jerusalem for the feast of Passover, and when he was twelve years old, they went up according to festival custom. After they had completed its days, as they were returning, the boy Jesus remained behind in Jerusalem, but his parents did not know it. Thinking that he was in the caravan, they journeyed for a day and looked for him among their relatives and acquaintances, but not finding him, they returned to Jerusalem to look for him. After three days they found him in the temple, sitting in the midst of the teachers, listening to them and asking them questions, and all who heard him were astounded at his understanding and his answers.

When his parents saw him, they were astonished, and his mother said to him, "Son, why have you done this to us? Your father and I have been looking for you with great anxiety."

And he said to them, "Why were you looking for me? Did you not know that I must be in my Father's house?" But they did not understand what he said to them.

He went down with them and came to Nazareth, and was obedient to them; and his mother kept all these things in her heart. And Jesus advanced [in] wisdom and age and favor before God and man.

Grieving the Loss of Health

Losing someone while they're alive is a different kind of sorrow than losing someone to death. Our needy beloved may be suffering from the loss of mental health, physical health, or cognition, but no matter what is "lost," we can empathize with Our Lady when Jesus went missing on the way home from Jerusalem. Years before, when Mary was hiding with her family in Egypt, at least she had Jesus with her, in her arms. But now, for the first time since the Incarnation in her womb, she had no idea where he even was.

It's like, when we love someone, we know what they're made for. We know what we want for them: life, and life abundantly. We want them to thrive. We want them to be whole, happy, and filled with meaning. Loving them — and being part of their existence in any way — is a tremendous privilege, and the greatest joy in sharing their lives is when we can celebrate that they are living fully.

Mary knew what Jesus was made for. She knew his destiny; she knew his origin. He was the King of kings. He was love himself!

Yet she also knew how short this world could fall in fulfilling that. She'd already tasted firsthand how selfish and evil this "valley of tears" could be. The minute she discovered that he wasn't safely with the caravan as she'd thought he was, she knew that he was vulnerable to all the dangers of this fallen world. She could no longer offer what limited protection she normally provided. And whatever happened to him, she wasn't there to share it — good or bad.

> I want to suffer and even rejoice for love, for this is my way of scattering flowers. Never a flower shall I find but its petals shall be scattered for you; and all the while I will sing; yes, always sing, even when gathering roses in the midst of thorns; and the longer and sharper the thorns may be, the sweeter shall be my song!
> — St. Thérèse of Lisieux, **The Story of a Soul**

I had a situation in which a loved one suffered a stroke, and by God's grace, he survived. His outlook was good. Nevertheless, I found myself shocked that I was weeping and crying for days, and unable to sleep well during the night. Shouldn't I be happy, I thought, that we have such a good prognosis? How can I be crying, when this needy beloved of mine could already be dead?

Fortunately, a wise doctor gave me some great advice. She told me that grief is not reserved for when somebody has died. One can grieve the loss of health. Looking at it that way made it much easier for me to accept the grief of this "loss." Instead of fighting against my sorrow, I worked my way through it, one day at a time.

When our needy beloved suffers a loss, we are well within our rights to grieve and feel sorrowful, just as Mary did. And now, as we walk through that loss, she walks with us, with as much intensity and feeling as she walked breathlessly through the streets of Jerusalem, seeking her beloved Son.

Risks and Tradeoffs, Even for Mary

Life has risks. Period. Within that, we take chances and make tradeoffs. Mary let Jesus out of her sight — perhaps to give him the "good" of spending time with extended family, or perhaps for some other reason. As she and Joseph searched for him for three days, did she regret this tradeoff? Or did she focus on the situation and do what needed to be done?

Mary is interesting. She loves as perfectly as a human being can love. She is without the stain of sin. Nevertheless, she lost track of Jesus. This was no sin; rather, it is a sign of our human limits. As much as she loved Jesus, she could not protect him from every danger or foresee every challenge. Indeed, it was not her task to do so. Her task had been to go on a pilgrimage to Jerusalem. Now, it was to find her Son.

Imagine what Mary must have felt, running through Jerusalem, describing her Son to strangers: "Have you seen this boy? Can you help me find him? He's just a child. He deserves to know he is safe. Does he have food to eat and shelter over his head?"

For a caregiver, discovering how to meet our loved one's needs is part of the journey. We look for ways to connect with, help, and delight them, facing our limitations at all times. We must make decisions: which treatment path to take, which purchases to prioritize, and how to take care of ourselves at the same time.

Many of these decisions have no clear answer, and no right answer. The burden of the responsibility is huge, and Mary knows how it feels. It can be frightening knowing that each moment that passes, our needy beloved could be suffering, or could become harder and harder to reach. Mary knew the same, that every hour in which she didn't find Jesus meant a greater chance that he had fallen into danger.

Great Anxiety

This led her to an emotion that many caregivers are familiar with: worry. In a June 2020 study, nearly one-third of caregivers reported mental or behavioral health problems such as anxiety, depression, or substance abuse. And it's no wonder. When a loved one seems to be in danger, the constant vigilance to their needs continues on, even when they are out of sight, as Jesus was when Mary and Joseph discovered him absent.

Mary actually uses the word *anxiety* when she finally confronts her Son. "Son, why have you done this to us? Your father and I have been looking for you with great anxiety" (Lk 2:48). For those of us who relate to this challenge, we see proof in Mary yet again that this is not a personal failing; if it were, the Queen of Peace herself would not have experienced it. Instead, this anxious vigilance is a suffering that Mary understands. She accompanies us through it.

Furthermore, we know that Jesus was missing for three days. Three days is a long time in such a state. It's long enough that I have to believe our others-centered, full-of-love parental role models did something not mentioned in the Bible: They ate; they drank water; and they rested to the extent they were able.

Mary and Joseph understood the brutal tradeoffs that must be made in a crisis situation. On the one hand, did they not yearn to seek their Son every single moment of the morning and night? On the other hand, did not their human limitations demand they care for themselves as well? Every moment in which they ate was a moment they could have been looking, and every moment in which they looked was a moment their energy stores depleted further.

People tell caregivers, "Be sure to practice self-care," but each caregiving situation is its own tightrope which balances very particular (and often contradictory) needs. Our Lady understands this constant balancing act. She's walked the tightrope. And I think it's clear that as she journeyed through Jerusalem looking for her Son, her hair was probably out of place. Her clothes were likely a bit disheveled. It's no stretch to think that she had bags under her eyes. There's no picture-perfect way to walk the tightrope. Like Our Lady, we walk it with "great anxiety."

Did You Not Know?

And yet, she *did* find Jesus. He'd been in the temple the whole time. "Did you not know that I must be in my Father's house?" (Lk 2:49).

Jesus' lax response to his parents' frantic search can strike us as insensitive, but it's also a huge relief. Jesus hadn't been taken by robbers on the way back to Galilee. He hadn't been starving or kidnapped. He hadn't been sold into slavery. He hadn't gotten ill or been bitten by a snake. He hadn't been lying by the side of the road wondering why oh why his mother hadn't found him yet because he was in dire straits.

He'd been in his Father's house. He'd been *exactly* where he was meant to be.

It's very possible that we are also exactly where we're meant to be. It's possible that *this* is all in the plan God has for my son's life, and for mine. Somehow, someway, all this suffering, all this frantic searching can be addressed with the simplicity of Jesus in the temple, "Did you not know that I must be in my Father's house?" Or in words that have been attributed to St. Teresa of Ávila, "You are exactly where you are meant to be."

Our Lady's sorrows force us to face this problem of suffering: Why does God's plan mean suffering for me and for my loved one? And just in the same way that the sorrows ask the question, they direct us to an answer, because we know how these stories end. Just as these sorrows end in glory, joy, and abundant life in heaven (and many, many mercies on earth) for (and because of) Jesus and Mary, so too can we trust that our sorrows will end this way as well. This is Jesus' promise. This is the good news he came to proclaim. "Seek and you will find" (Mt 7:7).

Conclusion

Our loved ones may get lost. One day, because of the circle of life, we will lose them for good, or they will lose us. Yet we can have true hope in that abundant, everlasting life, and we can even hope for mercies while we still live on this earth. I'm not saying it's easy. The point of this book is that it's *not* easy, it wasn't meant to be easy, and it never was easy, not even for Mary. In this very struggle we find our deepest connection with heaven. In this very sorrow, we find our solace. Here, in the uncertain confusion between Jerusalem and Nazareth, when we're not sure which end is up, we meet a woman who has walked this journey before and accompanies us now to help us look.

∼ *PRAYER* ∼

Our Lady of Sorrows, you never expected anything to go wrong on your way home from Jerusalem. Neither can I say that I expected the sorrows and loss that have occurred in my life. Be with me and help me focus on doing what needs to be done. Guard me against the snares of regret and despair. Pray for me, that I may have the hope to continue on when my journey feels discouraging. Mary, you found your Son in the temple. He was exactly where he was meant to be. Pray for my needy beloved, that he (she) may be exactly where God means him (her) to be, and that I too may walk the path God desires of me. Let me take courage in the words of your Son, that whatever is lost will be found. Pray that I may one day feel the joy of the woman who found her lost coin, and of you, who found your Son safe in Jerusalem. Amen.

Chapter Four

The Meeting of Mary with Jesus on His Way to Calvary

LIMITATION

The fourth Sorrow of Mary is her meeting Jesus on the *Via Dolorosa*. The *Stabat Mater* (printed on the following pages) is a thirteenth-century Catholic hymn that describes Mary's suffering during Jesus' crucifixion.

1. *Stabat mater dolorósa*
juxta Crucem lacrimósa,
dum pendébat Fílius.

At the Cross her station keeping,
Stood the mournful Mother weeping,
Close to Jesus to the last:

2. *Cuius ánimam geméntem,*
contristátam et doléntem
pertransívit ivide.

Through her heart, his sorrow sharing,
All his bitter anguish bearing,
Now at length the sword has pass'd.

3. *O quam tristis et afflícta*
fuit illa benedícta,
mater Unigéniti!

Oh, how sad and sore distress'd
Was that Mother highly blest
Of the sole-begotten One!

4. *Quae mœrébat et doléhat,*
pia Mater, dum vidébat
nati pœnas ínclyti.

Christ above in torment hangs;
She beneath beholds the pangs
Of her dying glorious Son.

5. *Quis est homo qui non fleret,*
matrem Christi si vidéret
in tanto supplício?

Is there one who would not weep,
Whelm'd in miseries so deep,
Christ's dear Mother to behold?

6. *Quis non posset contristári*
Christi Matrem contemplári
doléntem cum Fílio?

Can the human heart refrain
From partaking in her pain,
In that Mother's pain untold?

7. *Pro peccátis suæ gentis*
vidit Jésum in torméntis,
et flagéllis súbditum.

Bruis'd, derided, curs'd, defil'd,
She beheld her tender Child
All with bloody scourges rent;

8. *Vidit suum dulcem Natum*
moriéndo desolátum,
dum emísit spíritum.

For the sins of His own nation,
Saw Him hang in desolation,
Till His Spirit forth He sent.

9. *Eja, Mater, fons amóris*
me sentíre vim dolóris
fac, ut tecum lúgeam.

O thou Mother! Fount of love!
Touch my spirit from above,
Make my heart with thine accord:

10. *Fac, ut árdeat cor meum*
in amándo Christum Deum
ut sibi compláceam.

Make me feel as thou hast felt;
Make my soul to glow and melt
With the love of Christ my Lord.

11. *Sancta Mater, istud agas,*
crucifíxi fige plagas
cordi meo válide.

Holy Mother! Pierce me through;
In my heart each wound renew
Of my Saviour crucified:

12. *Tui Nati vulneráti,*
tam dignáti pro me pati,
pœnas mecum ivide.

Let me share with thee His pain,
Who for all my sins was slain,
Who for me in torments died.

13. *Fac me tecum pie flere,* | Let me mingle tears with thee,
crucifíxo condolére, | Mourning Him who mourn'd for me,
donec ego víxero. | All the days that I may live:

14. *Juxta Crucem tecum stare,* | By the Cross with thee to stay;
et me tibi sociáre | There with thee to weep and pray;
in planctu desídero. | Is all I ask of thee to give.
Amen. | Amen.

(Translation by Edward Caswall)

His Skin

How Mary must have suffered to observe that the angle of the cross on the way to Calvary threatened to drive a thorn into Jesus' head, and then — a moment later — to observe it happen! How she cried inside to witness that rather than get the treatment they needed, his wounds were being badly abused. Rather than being able to wrap them, she watched as pebbles ground themselves into the wounds of his knees, and the soldiers' whips snapped at a gash that was already wide open, red, and vulnerable.

Mary could only meet Jesus for a moment, yet his walk to

Calvary was long. Just as time — twenty years prior — must have seemed to stretch out when Mary and Joseph searched desperately for their lost Son in Jerusalem, so too must it have stretched out now when he approached her — and as they made him walk away.

Sometimes, when spiritual writers have written that Mary felt every one of Jesus' wounds as her own, I have wondered if they were not just spouting some Marian ideal, if they were projecting some fanciful notion onto her. But I understand this assertion in a new way as I tend to my needy beloved. I know what it feels like to be immersed in another's suffering: to "feel" the pain, frustration, and anger; to share sleeplessness; to live in that "unknown country" that lacks the consistent basics for self-care; to wonder how long it will last; to cry out to God; to hate this broken, ugly world; and to long for it all to be redeemed.

I cannot say how Mary's suffering compared to that of Jesus'; I'll leave that to the theologians. What I can say for sure is there's a lot of suffering. When the needy beloved suffers, the one who cares suffers too. But by God's grace, Jesus and Mary remind us of the end of the story. After the road to Calvary, after the crucifixion, after Jesus was taken down from the cross and placed in his mother's arms, and after the stone was rolled in front of the tomb, he rose.

Long Walk

This long, long walk of the needy beloved takes place in the middle of things. For Mary, she had three prior sorrows with which to get used to the idea that things weren't going to be easy, and after this sorrow, she will have three more to go. During the walk to Calvary, she may have felt as we may feel when our needy beloved is deep in suffering: that it has gone on a long time, and it feels like it will never end. And most of all, that it isn't right. That they deserve better.

Jesus deserved better, yet he took our place and that of our needy beloved so that what we're suffering right now can count for something. If he hadn't walked the road to Calvary, bloodied and sore, bearing that heavy cross and wearing the humiliating, painful crown, then all our suffering now would be for naught. But when everyone around him looked on him with hate, or ignored his pain and went about their business, or snapped the whip to hurt him more, he pressed on. He kept going.

> *Those who pray and suffer, leaving action for others, will not shine here on earth; but what a radiant crown they will wear in the kingdom of life! Blessed be the "apostolate of suffering"!*
> — *St. Josemaría Escrivá,* **The Way**

And when the only consolation Mary had was also an immense sorrow — meeting her Son on the torturous walk to his execution — she did not leave; she did not run away; she did not give in to despair. She pressed on. She kept going.

Because he endured through this suffering and sorrow, Jesus rose from the dead. He reversed the curse of original sin and opened up the gates of heaven. He sent the Holy Spirit to accompany us here on earth and breathed hope into our suffering world.

Those are the results of this sorrow. Mary could not have named them at the time. All she knew for sure was that her Son suffered before her eyes and there was little she could do. But she did what mattered most. She did as Jesus did: She pressed on. She kept going.

We cannot know what glory may amount from the suffering that has been heaped upon our needy loved one. We may be blessed to be able to comfort and help them more than Mary was able to do during Jesus' walk to Calvary. If this is the case, then let's do so! Every instance in which we tend to the wounds of our needy beloved, we tend to the wounds of Christ. We console Mary by doing what she was unable to do in that moment: bring the beloved water, soothe their fears, tend to their sores, and answer their cries.

O you souls who wish to go on with so much safety and consolation, if you knew how pleasing to God is suffering and how much it helps in acquiring other good things, you would never seek consolation in anything; but you would rather look upon it as a great happiness to bear the Cross of the Lord.
— *St. John of the Cross,* **Dark Night of the Soul**

In this way, when we tend to our needy beloved in the depths of their sufferings, we win two jewels for heaven: first, by consoling one of God's children, and second, by consoling our Wounded Savior.

In a similar way, our loved one's suffering can win two gems as well: first, by gaining whatever unknown glory their sufferings merit, and second (if they choose), by gaining intimacy with Our Savior, who shares with them the suffering of his walk to the cross.

But these meditations on heaven's joy may feel too intangible to bring comfort in the midst of suffering. In those moments, consider simply that Mary understands. She looks on your needy beloved with the same loving grief that she held for her Son on the Way of the Cross. She stands beside you on your needy beloved's journey. You can console each other.

Consolation That Her Presence
Could Console Him

In the midst of this great sorrow is a consolation, just as in the middle of a dark night, the stars provide tiny spots of illumination. That consolation is that Jesus was able to see Mary standing there. Her presence was a comfort to him, as it is for us now. Their meeting is not recorded in the Bible, but we know it happened from tradition. Their meeting was likely brief, soon after Christ's first nasty fall, and in that moment, Mary witnessed all the wretchedness that the people around her Son put him through. Yet, what was wretched for her was also a moment in which Jesus could see that he wasn't alone. Her presence showed him that someone loved him, that someone grieved his fate, and that Mary shared his suffering in her heart.

So even though Mary witnessed all the grotesque details of Jesus' torture, she perhaps saw, too, a glimmer of relief in his eyes — just for a moment — that she was there.

There are times when our presence is not enough to console our needy beloved. But in certain, beautiful moments, it can be. Even in the midst of the most difficult times, God offers us small graces. Like Mary, then, we can keep going.

Right after Mary and Jesus were forced to part, the soldiers recognized that he might not make it all the way to Golgotha

> *Stay with me, Lord ... for as poor as my soul is, I want it to be a place of consolation for You.*
> — *Prayer of Padre Pio after Holy Communion*

alone. I wonder if Mary saw Simon of Cyrene from behind, and saw him help Jesus carry the cross as she longed to do. This, too, was both a sorrow and a consolation, for now he had some help, but he was getting farther and farther from her, and closer and closer to death.

Isn't it funny how intimately sorrow and consolation are linked? The other side of sorrow is joy, and the other side of love is loss. In life, we walk the razor thin edge between the two sides, feeling both in their time as we wobble between them. Yet to flee one is to flee the other. We can accept joy in our lives only when we accept sorrow. We can accept love only when we also accept loss.

This is the drama of our fragile, human lives. Perhaps it is why Jesus told us to take up our crosses, that we may take up our joys in their time as well (see Mt 16:24). Perhaps it is why the man who avoided suffering "went away sad" (Mt 19:22).

Mary's sorrow is different than sadness. It is founded on faith, given momentum by hope, and is the interwoven brother of love. Sorrow is deep, like roots that probe deeper and deeper so that the tree above can bear abundant fruit. It is like the chaff that grows up with the grain; to remove sorrow now would threaten the harvest, but one day, God will separate the two (see Mt 3:12). Sorrow will be forgotten, and we'll be left with abundance and joy.

Conclusion

When Mary met Jesus on his Way of the Cross, the Resurrection was very near. Her earlier sorrows had prepared her for decades, but now, the world would be saved by sun-up on Sunday.

This is not to say that it would be easy; she still had to traverse three of her life's greatest sorrows. Nevertheless, it is a reminder to hold firm in faith that all will be used for good. Our entire lives, in the eyes of God, pass in the blink of an eye. Through our own eyes, time drags on in difficult moments, months, and years. How long the *Via Dolorosa* must have felt to Our Lady, and to Christ! How long must have felt the three hours on the cross! And how gloomy and dark the three days before joy finally split through the darkness on Easter Sunday!

The days feel long. The nights, perhaps, even longer.

Nevertheless, we can count on the dawn breaking through, because God has promised it. We can count on all these sor-

> *The Lord sometimes makes you feel the weight of the cross. Although the weight seems intolerable, you are able to carry it, because the Lord, in his love and mercy, extends a hand to you and gives you strength.*
> *— Attributed to Padre Pio*

rows being used for good. Our faith tells us it is so, and we see Mary's sorrows as a prime example.

When the dawn has yet to break, we can look for stars. And when clouds obscure the night, we press on as Mary did, trusting they exist.

∼ *PRAYER* ∼

Our Lady of Sorrows, you met your Son on his painful walk to his death on Calvary. As I accompany my suffering loved one, please pray that I may be filled with your faith to trust in God's plan. Accompany me as I accompany my loved one. Pray that my presence may offer my needy beloved some consolation, as your presence did for Christ. Unite my needy beloved's suffering with that of Jesus, and unite my sorrow with yours, that this time may be of great use in heaven. For now, sorrow is interwoven with my love. Help me to accept this sorrow as you accepted the "sword" which pierced your soul. For love of you, Mother, and for love of our God, please send my needy beloved consolation along his (her) journey, that he (she) may carry his (her) cross with faith that his (her) work will be redeemed. Amen.

Chapter Five
The Death of Jesus
SURRENDER

The fifth Sorrow of Mary is the crucifixion of Jesus on Calvary, described here from the Gospel of John 19:16–30:

> So they took Jesus, and carrying the cross himself he went out to what is called the Place of the Skull, in Hebrew, Golgotha. There they crucified him, and with him two others, one on either side, with Jesus in the middle. Pilate also had an inscription written and put on the

cross. It read, "Jesus the Nazorean, the King of the Jews." Now many of the Jews read this inscription, because the place where Jesus was crucified was near the city; and it was written in Hebrew, Latin, and Greek. So the chief priests of the Jews said to Pilate, "Do not write 'The King of the Jews,' but that he said, 'I am the King of the Jews.'" Pilate answered, "What I have written, I have written."

When the soldiers had crucified Jesus, they took his clothes and divided them into four shares, a share for each soldier. They also took his tunic, but the tunic was seamless, woven in one piece from the top down. So they said to one another, "Let's not tear it, but cast lots for it to see whose it will be," in order that the passage of scripture might be fulfilled [that says]:

> "They divided my garments among them,
> and for my vesture they cast lots."

This is what the soldiers did. Standing by the cross of Jesus were his mother and his mother's sister, Mary the wife of Clopas, and Mary of Magdala. When Jesus saw his mother and the disciple there whom he loved, he said to his mother, "Woman, behold, your son." Then he said to the disciple, "Behold, your mother." And from that hour the disciple took her into his home.

After this, aware that everything was now finished, in order that the scripture might be fulfilled, Jesus said, "I thirst." There was a vessel filled with common wine. So they put a sponge soaked in wine on a sprig of hyssop and put it up to his mouth. When Jesus had taken the wine, he said, "It is finished." And bowing his head, he handed over the spirit.

I Thirst

My grandmother was in outpatient hospice for two years. At certain points, she was doing so well that she happily reported they threatened to kick her out of the program. Other times were more difficult.

Her children and nurses kept her on a medicinal schedule, yet one of the drugs had an unfortunate side effect: It dried out my grandmother's mouth, making it difficult for her to speak. Water glasses were too heavy for her to lift on her own, so we lifted her cup to her lips. Yet swallowing the liquid hurt her throat.

One hospice nurse had a clever solution. She pulled out a pack of small blue sponges, which were attached to small sticks like lollipops. We dipped the sponges in water, and when my grandmother's mouth dried out, gave her a tiny "drink" from the sponge. It provided her parched tongue and lips a little moisture.

I remember that now, when I consider Christ on the cross, crying out, "I thirst." The soldiers put some vinegar on a sponge on a stick and lifted it to him to drink.

Christ's "thirst" on the cross can be interpreted very deeply and spiritually, yet even on its most practical level, it hits home. We may not know what it feels like to be whipped, or to wear a crown of thorns, or to be crucified, but who among us has never been thirsty?

> *The closer we come to Jesus, the better we will know his thirst.*
> — *Mother Teresa, Letter to the Missionaries of Charity Sisters, July 29, 1993*

For years, Mary had been the one to answer her Son's thirsty cry. In his infancy, she had answered this need from her very body, nursing him until he was nourished and satisfied. Now, she looked on helplessly from the foot of the cross. Her Son thirsted, but she was powerless to give him drink.

This is a sorrow which grieves me deeply: that I hear the cry of my needy beloved, but my power to answer that cry does not fully address his need. All our work to tend to them merely mitigates *some* of the suffering but does not make it disappear completely. How Mary must have longed to carry that cross instead of Christ! How quickly she would have jumped onto the cross in his place! But she could not, and neither can we.

And just as Jesus was meant to experience the passion in order to bring about salvation, so Mary was meant not to. She was meant to stand there powerless at the bottom of the cross. In her limitation, she fulfilled her role. She could not give Jesus a drink, but she did stand at his feet.

There were moments in which Mary's role was active: She said yes at the Annunciation, she took charge with Joseph in keeping Jesus safe in Egypt, she prompted Jesus to perform his first miracle at Cana, and on and on. Yet now, her role was to remain with him. She could not take away his pain, yet she was just as much a part of the good that God was doing through his passion because of her presence. She is the Co-redemptrix. She redeemed the world *with* Christ, despite how powerless she was now to answer his physical thirst.

Sometimes, our needy beloved has needs we can't meet. They carry a cross that no one else can carry for them, as much as we want to.

Thanks be to God that Our Lady understands, and that we can have hope in Christ that good will come out of bad, that joy will come out of sorrow, as it did for Jesus and Mary.

Behold Your Son

We all know that denial is the first stage of grief, and I wonder if Mary was at all in this stage when Jesus addressed her from the cross. What a pang of dismay she must have felt at first when he gestured to John, "the disciple … whom he loved," and said, "Woman, behold, your son" (Jn 19:26).

On the one hand, to Mary's dismay, Jesus was giving her a replacement for him, someone to take care of her needs while she remained here on earth, since he was to go on. Of course, Mary would rather not need a replacement at all. She wanted Jesus, and no one else.

On the other hand, John himself was a gift to Mary. He *would* take care of her, and moreover, he was specifically chosen by Mary's own Son. In sorrow and love, so much is bittersweet.

When meditating on the Seven Sorrows of Mary, we have the privilege of imagining ourselves in any number of roles. Sometimes, we can imagine what Mary would have felt. Other times, what Jesus would have felt. We can choose from any of the people around them and "walk in their shoes" during the meditation on the sorrow. Furthermore, we can imagine that Mary weeps for us or for our beloved, or that Jesus suffers with us or with our loved one. We can console Mary. We can console Christ. Either can console us or our needy one. The depths of the meditation are endless, yet for now, when I meditate on "Behold your son," I cannot help but ask Our Lady to behold my needy beloved as her own. I beg her to comfort him and to give him grace. Her love for my beloved needy one, perfectly reflecting Christ's, exceeds even my own which is so great that I can't begin to describe it.

"Behold your son," I beg her, that she may dip into the well of God's grace and consolation when my abilities fail to meet my loved one's "thirst." "Behold your son," when I don't know how to proceed, when my next steps are clouded and frustration mounts. "Behold your son," because offering my needy beloved to Mary in effect offers the same to Christ.

Just before her first sorrow, Mary presented the infant Jesus to God the Father in the temple. In this fifth sorrow, we imitate her, relying on her for our needy beloved as Jesus relied on her for John.

Our mortal limits will fail to satisfy our beloved's needs, but heaven has no such limits. There is no better place for our loved ones (or for ourselves) than in the care of Our Lady.

Pain and suffering have come into your life, but remember pain, sorrow, suffering are but the kiss of Jesus — a sign that you have come so close to Him that he can kiss you.
— Mother Teresa, **Life in the Spirit**

Shifting perspectives, we can see that Jesus does not only offer our needy beloved into Mary's hands, but he offers us as well. In what safer place can we find ourselves than in her womb with Christ? How can we walk this journey more safely than with our Mother at our side? She welcomes us as she welcomed John, embracing us fully as her own.

In sorrow and love, so much is bittersweet, for — offered to Mary in this deep sorrow — how can we but rejoice?

The Thieves at Christ's Side

I wonder what Mary made of the two thieves who hung at either side of her Son. For my part, I see in them reflections of myself when facing sorrow.

The temptation niggles in my mind to rebuke God for allowing my loved one to suffer. If he is so powerful and loving, the jaded logic goes, why doesn't God spare my needy beloved from this fate? In the same vein as this snarky temptation, one of the criminals beside him mocked Jesus, saying, "Are you not the Messiah? Save yourself and us" (Lk 23:39).

The criminal on Christ's other side took this same tone at first, as we see in the Gospel of Mark. "Those who were crucified with him also kept abusing him" (Mk 15:32).

Yet by and by, he changed his tune. He even chastised his

fellow robber, whose mockery he had previously joined. Turning to Jesus before he died, he said, "Jesus, remember me when you come into your kingdom" (Lk 23:42).

Jesus answered, "Amen, I say to you, today you will be with me in Paradise" (Lk 23:43).

By tradition, we call this second criminal Saint Dismas, and I like to remember his conversion when my faith during sorrow does not feel as unshakable as Our Lady's.

Rather than standing sorrowfully at Christ's feet, sometimes I fancy myself to be crucified as well in my caregiving, and the moment itself determines to which criminal I most relate.

Fortunately for Saint Dismas, he had the advantage during his execution of nothing less than the presence of Christ. So too did Mary during this fifth sorrow. So too do we.

In our sorrow, when we feel all but spent, when we feel that we are hanging onto one last unraveling strand of rope, God's grace is greater than our weakness. He is with us. He will determine, in his goodness, when to grant us that grace which he gave to Saint Dismas — that grace to see our suffering for the gift that it is, and to see Christ for who *he* is (the One who will transform it into a gift).

Though our life turns upside down, and our wells of strength run dry, we can pray these seven Hail Marys. When we remem-

> *It is by [Mary] that [Jesus] applies His merits to His members, and that He communicates His virtues, and distributes His graces. She is His Mysterious canal; she is His aqueduct, through which He makes His mercies flow gently and abundantly.*
>
> — *St. Louis de Montfort,* **True Devotion to Mary: With Preparation for Total Consecration**

ber Mary, she remembers us, and whomever she remembers, Christ remembers, too.

The robbers at Christ's side did not see the true nature of the man between them. They did not see him as Mary did. And whichever way we view our sufferings (and God) at this very moment, we can observe in this sorrow our situation: Christ is present. He suffers and dies for us. Mary is present too, and God's grace triumphs over all.

Conclusion

When we face our own "thirst," and that of our needy beloved; when we find ourselves deciding how to face our sorrows and our God like the robbers crucified with Christ; and when we offer ourselves and our loved ones into the generous hands of Our Lady; we know that our lives are closer than ever to the passion of Christ and the Sorrows of Our Lady.

Not only are we not alone, but we are privileged beyond our understanding to venture so close to the moment that changed the world. Our presence here will not be forgotten. Rather, we will be remembered and redeemed when we ask, like Saint Dismas, and when we entrust ourselves to Mary, like Saint John.

Mary watched her Son's execution with a sorrow that we begin to imagine when we accompany her in meditation.

At three o'clock, Jesus died. In that sorrowful hour, God himself darkened the world, yet before long a new day would dawn, a day more glorious than Dismas or John could imagine that bleak Friday. When our world darkens, we remember that Easter Sunday soon came, though there's no way to hurry it along.

Until then, we live this human life, with all its ups and downs. We wait and weep at the foot of the cross. We stand with Mary in the dark.

∽ *PRAYER* ∽

Here are two versions of a prayer to Our
Lady, inspired by her fifth sorrow.

For a male loved one

With confidence, Our Lady of Sorrows, I lay
my loved one at your feet and pray:
When his team discerns his care plan, behold your son.
When I feel I can do no more, behold your son.
When earthly help fails, behold your son.
When his consolations fall short, behold your son.
When he wakes in the night, behold your son
When he struggles by day, behold your son.
When he feels alone, behold your son.
When he is tempted to despair, behold your son.
When he struggles to endure, behold your son.
When his body betrays him, behold your son.
Mother of Mercy, behold your son.
Queen of Compassion, behold your son.
By morning, noon, and night, behold your son,
And lavish on him the grace of your Divine Child
That, united in Jesus' cross now, he may yet thrive in the abundance

For which he was made. Amen.

For a female loved one

With confidence, Our Lady of Sorrows, I lay
my loved one at your feet and pray:
When her team discerns her care plan, behold your daughter.
When I feel I can do no more, behold your daughter.
When earthly help fails, behold your daughter.
When her consolations fall short, behold your daughter.
When she wakes in the night, behold your daughter.
When she struggles by day, behold your daughter.
When she feels alone, behold your daughter.
When she is tempted to despair, behold your daughter.
When she struggles to endure, behold your daughter.
When her body betrays her, behold your daughter.
Mother of Mercy, behold your daughter.
Queen of Compassion, behold your daughter.
By morning, noon, and night, behold your daughter,
And lavish on her the grace of your Divine Child
That, united in Jesus' cross now, she may yet thrive in the abundance
For which she was made. Amen.

Chapter Six

The Piercing of the Side of Jesus and His Descent from the Cross

GRIEF

The sixth Sorrow of Mary is Jesus being taken down from the cross, described here in Matthew 27:57–58:

When it was evening, there came a rich man from Arimathea named Joseph, who was himself a disciple of Jesus. He went to Pilate and asked for the body of Jesus; then Pilate ordered it to be handed over.

St. Alphonsus Liguori, in an excerpt from his work *The Glories of Mary*, describes a private revelation that tradition holds was given to Saint Bridget about this moment in history:

It was revealed to Saint Bridget, that to take down the body of Jesus, three ladders were placed against the cross. Those holy disciples first drew out the nails from the hands and feet, and according to Metaphrastes, gave them in charge to Mary. Then one supported the upper part of the body of Jesus, the other the lower, and thus took it down from the cross. Bernardino de Bustis describes the afflicted mother as raising herself, and extending her arms to meet her dear Son; she embraces him, and then sits down at the foot of the cross. She sees his mouth open, his eyes shut, she examines the lacerated flesh, and those exposed bones; she takes off the crown, and sees the cruel injury made by those thorns, in that sacred head; she looks upon those pierced hands and feet, and says: Ah, my Son, to what has the love thou didst bear to men reduced thee! But what evil have thou done to them, that they have treated thee so cruelly?

The *Pietà*

We all know the image of Michelangelo's *Pietà*: Jesus' Body is draped over his mother's arm. For many of us, this is our first exposure to thinking about any of Mary's Seven Sorrows. At any rate, it was for me.

I don't know where I acquired it, but somehow a small *Pietà* figurine came into my possession. I kept it in a box in the closet with my holy cards and broken rosaries. It didn't see much sunlight in my house for a while. That is, until I really needed it.

My first pregnancy ended in miscarriage, and after my baby died, I thought I was doing pretty OK. But eventually, denial erodes into grief.

I took some time off work and found myself staring at this little figurine: There was a mother, like me, cradling her dead child in her arms. There wasn't much else to my meditation at the time. I just looked and looked at her and Jesus.

The figurine came out of the closet. I put it on a side table where I'd see it many times each day.

I didn't have much to say to Mary at that point. I still hadn't "found" the Seven Sorrows for my life. Nevertheless, there she was. There was my sorrow. There was my pain. It was all wrapped into one of the most pivotal moments in my history and in that of the world. But at that point, it all felt small and quiet, like this little figurine.

Space for Silence

This moment — the *Pietà* — is not the end. It is a heart-wrenching, sorrowful moment when everything changes, and the grief process kicks into high gear.

I asked a fellow mother, who had also experienced a miscarriage, "Does it ever get better?"

The phone went silent for a moment. "No," she said, "the pain is always there."

At the time, her answer gave me some kind of twisted comfort: In a way, keeping that sorrow meant keeping my child in the barest way, and my love along with it. Now, looking back, my experience strays from my friend's. The love stays, but the pain changes. Grief takes time. It loops in a unique, non-linear trajectory to peace.

Yet in the thick of it, in that stillness after the final breath, what can we do but keep silence? We ought not rush through grief; Mary certainly didn't.

After his death, Mary looks into the face of her crucified Son. She holds him. She takes that time with him, and with us.

We'll sit together here. We'll wait a while in this stillness.

Our hearts grieve.

And Mary grieves with us.

If you haven't already taken the plunge and prayed the Seven Sorrows of Mary, I encourage you to do so now. Or, if you've already begun this devotion in your life, set down this book and pray the Sorrows for today now, even if it is not when you normally pray them. Spend some time with Our Lady as she grieves over her Son's broken Body. "Watch and pray" (Mt 26:41).

The "Stigmata" of Our Lady

Ever since I first heard about the *stigmata* as a child, I couldn't feel

For some of us, spending time in silent meditation can be a challenge, which is one reason why the Seven Sorrows devotion, and the devotion of the Rosary, can be so helpful. As we greet Mary and ask for her prayers through the memorized Hail Mary, we can actually allow the Hail Mary which we're reciting to fade into the background (so to speak) of our meditation. With the Hail Mary as the "background music" to our prayer, we can allow our thoughts to drift to the sorrow or mystery on which we are meditating.

but awe at those saints who experienced it. The *stigmata* are the miraculous presence of one or more of Christ's wounds on a person's body. Padre Pio, to give a modern saint as an example, wore black gloves every day to cover the miraculous holes in his hands, and he bled through the gloves while saying Mass. How particularly chosen must Padre Pio have been to be given such an intimate way to relate to Christ, especially during the moment of his passion! How privileged he was to be given that blessing!

On the other hand, Our Lady received no outward mark of her suffering. Her sorrows were interior. Or, when they were shown, they were marked on her needy Beloved, and not on her own self. How she grieved to count his wounds when she held his Body in her arms!

Gratitude for suffering is a precious jewel for our heavenly crown … man should always firmly believe that God sends just that trial which is most beneficial for him.
— Attributed to St. Gertrude the Great

Through this lens, when our deepest sorrows echo Our Lady's Seven Sorrows, we experience — in a sense — the "stigmata" of Our Lady. It is through this vantage point that I can begin to comprehend what the saints meant when they considered suffering a privilege: How particularly chosen must we be to experience these parallel sorrows of Our Lady!

Our sorrows need not be isolated sufferings that serve no purpose. Rather, God will use them for his purposes, which can only be good. Furthermore, they indicate to us how deeply he desires our closeness to him, and to his Blessed Mother.

Lest we be deceived, this gift of Our Lady's sorrowful "stigmata" is not a sign of the holiness of the recipient, but rather an invitation. Its closeness to Our Lady, and to the passion, shows the depth of the love God has for the sufferer. It's an invitation of the most personal kind.

When we offer our sorrows to Our Lady, and meditate on her sorrows, we say yes to that invitation. What follows will best be known by the sufferer, Our Lady, and God, as the relationship deepens and love grows.

Conclusion

Our Lady experienced incredible sorrow after watching her Son wrongfully die. She held space for her grief, and we can too. At the same time, Mary never despaired. She grieved, sorrowed, and held out hope, all at the same time.

We can unite our grief and fear to Our Lady's and beg her to distribute the grace of hope into our hearts during our darkest times. Though dead, Christ had not abandoned Mary, and though we cannot see him, he has not abandoned us either. He is working great things for us and our needy beloved, that in his time, we may see the glorious resolution of his plans revealed.

In the meantime, we keep silence with Our Lady, wait in hope, and entrust ourselves and our needy beloved to Divine Mercy.

∼ *PRAYER* ∼

Our Lady of Sorrows, after Jesus died, you held his precious Body in your arms. So, too, hold my needy beloved in your arms now, during his (her) sorrow, and at the hour of his (her) death. And hold me in the same way. Present our sorrows humbly to God that he may give us true faith in the redemption that Christ made possible by the death he suffered. May God redeem us and all our sufferings, and may we remain forever close to you and to your Son. Amen.

Chapter Seven
The Burial of the Body of Jesus
HOPE OR DESPAIR

The seventh Sorrow of Mary is the burial of Jesus by Joseph of Arimathea, described here in Matthew 27:59–66:

Taking the body, Joseph wrapped it [in] clean linen and laid it in his new tomb that he had hewn in the rock. Then he rolled a huge stone across the entrance to the tomb and departed. But Mary Magdalene and the other Mary remained sitting there, facing the tomb.

The next day, the one following the day of preparation, the chief priests and the Pharisees gathered before Pilate and said, "Sir, we remember that this impostor while still alive said, 'After three days I will be raised up.' Give orders, then, that the grave be secured until the third day, lest his disciples come and steal him and say to the people, 'He has been raised from the dead.' This last imposture would be worse than the first." Pilate said to them, "The guard is yours; go secure it as best you can." So they went and secured the tomb by fixing a seal to the stone and setting the guard.

Him Whom My Soul Loves

In Mary's third sorrow, when Jesus went missing in Jerusalem, Mary sought him out like the lover in the Song of Songs: " 'Let me rise then and go about the city, through the streets and squares; Let me seek him whom my soul loves.' I sought him but I did not find him" (3:2). Now, however, Mary knows where her Son's Body lies. She knows, yet she cannot find him because his soul isn't there. This time, Mary must be the one to leave.

Joseph of Arimathea and other disciples helped usher Jesus'

Body to the tomb. The women, per tradition, prepared his Body for burial as quickly as they could; time was scarce as Passover approached. Which disciple would have been the one to tell Mary that now she must leave Jesus' Body there in the cold, stone chamber? Who could have dared watch her face as they rolled the stone to seal the tomb?

A New Jerusalem (In More Ways than One)

Jesus went missing in Jerusalem for three days; now he would remain dead for the very same length of time. Yet how different the experience for Mary! In both cases, Jesus was going about his Father's work, and in both cases, he wasn't *actually* lost to Mary — not at all! — he was, as he'd explained, in his Father's house. "Did you not know?" he had asked her at the time, when as a child he stayed behind in the temple.

The Bible reminds us that from the very beginning, Mary "kept all these things, reflecting on them in her heart" (Lk 2:19). She considered the things her Son said and did; she considered the words of the angel Gabriel, and of Scripture. We also see that throughout his ministry, Jesus openly shared again and again that he would be put to death, and after three days would rise again. It got to a point where Peter scolded him for saying it (see Mt 16:21–22)! Therefore, it is no big reach to assume that Mary had heard Jesus say those things too.

I wonder then, as she grieved at the tomb, if she grieved as one who has lost everything, or if she grieved differently. Humanity had just savagely discarded the greatest gift it had ever been given and its only chance to reverse the damning mistake of Adam and Eve. Mary had witnessed the greatest cruelty to the most innocent and selfless of beings. She had seen the victory of selfishness over love itself. To have to live in such a world! No wonder Jesus told the women on the way to Calvary, "Do not weep for me; weep instead for yourselves and for your children" (Lk 23:28).

On the other hand, Mary remembered. She had listened carefully to Jesus' every word. So did she grieve remembering the lessons of Jerusalem, the messages of the angel, and the mysterious sayings of her Son? Did she grieve as one who still held that last candle of hope? Did she grieve like the wise virgins — those who kept enough oil (read: hope!) in their lamps to await the bridegroom (see Mt 25:1–13)? Did she suspect that despite all the evils which had taken place, the final word was not yet spoken?

Sorrow and Grief, Not Despair

I have to believe that Mary remembered enough — and she trusted enough — to believe that not all was lost. If she'd simply done the cold calculations without faith or hope, how could she but despair? Mary, better than anyone else, knew what was at stake. Humans had just killed God. Sin had killed love. What greater darkness could there be?

But Mary is not one for cold calculations. She embraced the totality of reality, which includes, of course, the love of her Son.

Who knows to what extent she imagined that Jesus would return to her in the flesh? Who knows if she could have foretold her Son's appearance in a glorified Body, the descent of the Holy Spirit in tongues of fire at Pentecost, or her own Assumption into heaven?

All I know is that she kept that allegorical lantern of hope lit. And wouldn't you know it? The Bridegroom did show up, for her and for all of us.

The Caregiver's Battle

Loving and caring for a person who is suffering can tempt us to despair. We can despair about their pain, their mortality, our own challenges, our limitations, and on and on. There is no topic that the Devil won't twist into despair if given the chance.

At the tomb, Mary shows us an alternative to despair. Grief and sorrow can be healthy and holy. In fact, carrying our sorrow with hope, as Mary did, leaves room for miracles. Only when our lamps are lit can we see the bridegroom coming.

In the greatest challenges of every life, hope is most essential. Our greatest stories tell tales of holding on and pressing forward, even when all seems lost. Some days and nights, when sleep is scarce and anxiety runs high, we may be tempted to make cold calculations about our loved ones' situations. We may let fear get the better of us. We may let negative thoughts take hold.

When this happens, run to Mary. She has stood at the tomb at the end of the world and crushed the serpent under her feet. She suspected the other side (the Resurrection side, the love side, God's side) of Jesus' crucifixion, and she sees the other side of our needy beloved's sufferings too. She knows the love being poured down upon your loved one. She sees the glories yet to come for them. She sees the miracles to come on earth (great and tiny alike) of which now you can have no suspicion.

We don't know what tomorrow will look like for a loved one who suffers or for we who sorrow along with them, but if we can ask for the grace to keep alive one tiny ember of hope, then we can stand at the tomb with Our Lady and weep. We can weep — and one day will blink to see Christ approaching through the tears.

Conclusion

When we face our greatest sorrows, and in those moments when all seems lost, Our Lady remembers us. She was there at the tomb when the cold, heavy stone separated her from her needy Beloved, ostensibly forever. But God overturns our fears. He gives us a grace, a sliver, a way. What remains for us to do is to keep that hope, to use our reason, and to learn from history: Let us learn from Mary's third sorrow, and let us learn from the Third Day after her seventh sorrow. Jesus rose! Alleluia!

He proved to us — yet again — that his love and power overcome our human conclusions. No matter how dire our situation may be, the situation cannot have the final word as long as we hold out hope in God's love for us. Things may not turn out the way we would like, but they cannot be in vain when we unite our circumstances to the cross of Christ and the sorrows of Mary. They cannot be in vain with the Blessed Mother at our side, she who loves us as her own.

> *[Mary] acts as a mediatrix not as an outsider, but in her position as mother. … She also wishes the messianic power of her Son to be manifested, that salvific power of his which is meant to help man in his misfortunes, to free him from the evil which in various forms and degrees weighs heavily upon his life.*
> *— Pope St. John Paul II,* **Redemptoris Mater**

$\sim$ *PRAYER* $\sim$

Our Lady of Sorrows, guard me and my needy beloved from despair, today and always. By God's grace, remind me of God's past mercies toward me and the ones whom I love. Help me remember that all is in God's hands, and that he has a plan to redeem it all. In my sorrow, Mother Mary, help me not to give way to cold calculations. Instead, beg Jesus on my behalf. Beg him to break through this night with the light of his love, that I may always trust in the incalculable mercy of God. Amen.

Conclusion

If you have read this far, you have dipped your toe into the exceedingly vast spiritual treasure which is devotion to Our Lady of Sorrows. The work you have done in reading and in praying (as well as in your caregiving!) is good and important work, which God does not take lightly.

To the contrary, God values meditations on Christ's passion and on Our Lady's Seven Sorrows very much. As caregivers, we have a privileged perspective on the reason why: Caregiving tends to limit our resources financially, temporally, physically, and so on. As a result, our social circles tend to shrink. Not only do everyday needs demand a less involved schedule, but acquaintances and friends often distance themselves when they do not understand either our lack of engagement or how to respond to this new great need. For this reason, during times of crisis, little acts of remembrance mean a great deal. When we remember Mary in her caregiving and her sorrow, it means a great deal to her as well.

Twice, during our tough time of caregiving, some friends left us a basket of vegetables and fruit on our front porch. I will never forget that. Neither will I forget those who responded with kind words when I shared a diagnosis I was still processing. Nor those who offered — and provided — practical help. I feel a loyalty to these persons greater than that which I have ever felt before, because in our time of need, they showed up.

Mercies Not Forgotten

Is it any wonder then that this is the measure by which Christ will judge us at the end of time? "For I was hungry and you gave me food, I was thirsty and you gave me drink, a stranger and you welcomed me, naked and you clothed me, ill and you cared for me, in prison and you visited me" (Mt 25:35–36). Or is it any wonder that meditating on the passion means so much to Our Lord? Jesus told St. Maria Faustina, "The contemplation of My painful wounds is of great profit to you, and it brings Me great joy."

What better way to show up for Christ than to meditate on his passion in the arms of his Blessed Mother? Who better to share with us her sorrow and the sufferings of Our Lord? It is no wonder, then, that Mary can promise us rewards for this remembrance in heaven, because she knows — as we know — that those who care for the caregiver and the needy beloved are embraced as treasures.

In our suffering and sorrow, God's will allows us to be for Mary and Jesus what we need for ourselves, and for them to be for us that understanding company which we so desire.

Our Lady will not forget us when we accompany her in her Seven Sorrows. Neither will her Son.

So as we cry from our own burdens like Saint Dismas, "Jesus, remember me when you come into your kingdom," we can have true faith and take great hope in Christ's answer, "Today, you will be with me in Paradise."

On the Needy Beloved

In this book, we have walked with Mary through her Seven Sorrows as she walks with us in our caregiving journeys. She is witness to the fact that God uses our sorrows which spring from love for another. He uses this sorrow and love for good — a good greater than we can imagine. We have placed our trust in Jesus and Mary to accompany us in this likely-unexpected mission we now undertake. We turn to them in our hearts, receiving and offering consolation as God allows.

Mary's example shatters myths about what perfection is supposed to look like. She combats seven lies which threaten to ensnare us during our toughest times. When we meditate on her Seven Sorrows, not only do we understand the powerful truths that crush the lies, but we also receive a promise of heavenly gifts which will be bestowed upon us for the devotion.

We met Mary at that heavy moment in which Simeon prophesied the sufferings her Son would face. In the Seven Sorrows devotion, she shares with us that sense of dread and fear that we too may face when discovering what our loved one's suffering might mean for them. We accompanied Mary in that painful promise which Simeon made her, that a sword would pierce her heart. When we have felt our own hearts pierced with love for one who suffers, we have offered it to Mary and asked her to remain close to us and to our needy beloved.

We journeyed with Mary into Egypt, as death chased her, Joseph, and their needy Beloved. She, likewise, has walked with us as we attempt to flee great dangers to our needy beloved's quality of life. We have felt as strangers "in a foreign land," but not fully alone — as we walk here with Our Lady and with Jesus.

We share with Mary our "great anxiety" as the fate of our needy beloved is yet unknown, and as we seek out ways to strengthen and comfort our needy beloved as they walk the road before them. Like Mary and Joseph who searched for Jesus in Jerusalem, there is much we do not know which we wish to know, and much we do not have which we wish to have. With Mary, we learned that God is in control, and that despite all the sorrows, our loved ones are — as Jesus was — exactly where they are meant to be. With Mary we have entrusted our needy beloved to the Lord, carrying still great grief and sorrow in our hearts.

We have watched our needy beloved suffer, just as Mary watched Jesus suffer as he was forced to carry the cross to Golgotha. We have been helpless, just as Mary was, to carry our needy beloved's burden for them. We have been helpless to walk their roads. Yet with admiration, and whatever limited consolation we can offer, we accompany them. Mary has looked lovingly and sorrowfully upon our needy beloved as well. She has accompanied us, as we accompany them, down the dark and rocky terrain of this "valley of tears."

With Our Lady, we have tended to our needy beloved. They thirst, they hunger, they cry, and we answer as best we are able, knowing that it does not address the depth of the thirst they have for healing and life. Mary waits with us, with them. With Mary, we have cried out for God to help our needy beloved, and to help us, and we have asked for grace to believe, like Saint Dismas, that despite all appearances, everything — even this — will be used for good.

We have wept in silence with Our Lady of Sorrows, remembering her grief as she held her Son's corpse in her arms. We have sat with her — and she has sat with us — when we have no thoughts to put together, no strength to take any actions, but only a great sorrow in which to abide. For in grief, the only way out is through, and Mary goes through with us. She has walked this way before. We have meditated on that moment for her and have thus offered her some consolation.

Finally, we have stood with Mary as some brave disciple told her it was time to step away from the tomb. We have watched her step back from Christ's Body and be cut off from him. We have wondered with her whether that was the end, or whether more was in store. We have spiritually battled the temptations to doubt and despair. Through it all, she has been with us too.

As we have meditated on Mary's Seven Sorrows, we have been blessed to share our grief with Mary as well. We have — in meditating on her sorrow — an important opportunity to grow deeply close to the Blessed Mother, and she extends a hand to grow close with us during a time when we may need it most.

This book has attempted to shed light on some of the caregiver's spiritual journey, and I can attest that God has done enormous work on my soul through this phase of life and through devotion to Our Lady of Sorrows. This gives me great joy for my own sake, and also for my needy beloved's.

If the suffering of Jesus in his crucifixion shocked and horrified, so too does his glorious resurrection shock and delight. If the suffering we face now nabbed us more suddenly and fully than we could have ever expected, so too can we expect that its spiritual outcome will fill our lives with more joy than we ever saw coming.

We may not feel like an "Easter people" during our sorrows, but neither do we deny the end of Mary's story: Her beloved Son triumphed. All his suffering was turned into goodness. She herself was consoled and now rejoices in heaven.

As this book has attempted to show, when we carry sorrow, Our Lady accompanies us through it and invites us to join her in hers. Moreover, God himself extends an invitation to embrace his Mother, and to practice love even as she did. The end is nothing less than a close and eternal unity with God.

And when all that seems too lofty, we can simply remember: Jesus and Mary walk with us.

Starting a Support Group

Prayerfully consider consoling fellow caregivers with a support group. A support group can be as casual as you and a fellow caregiver meeting over the phone, or as formal as a group at your parish! Here are a few ideas for getting started:

- Reach out to your parish to ask for help spreading the word in the bulletin or in an announcement after Mass.
- Contact OSV for information about bulk discounts of this book which may be available for your parish.
- Find a schedule of meetings that works for your participants. You might choose to meet once a

week for ten weeks or once a month for nearly a year, to cover one chapter per meeting.

- Consider the advantages of meeting in person (opportunities for hugs and comforted tears) or virtually (easier logistics for busy caregivers) or a hybrid of the two.

- Begin each meeting by praying the Seven Sorrows of Mary together. Then, discuss the sorrow of the week using the questions at the end of each chapter. Take time to listen to each other and encourage each other. Feel free to conclude with the prayer provided at the end of each chapter as well.

- Don't forget to provide tissues!

TIP: Communicate with the extraordinary ministers of the Eucharist at your parish. Caregivers (and their needy beloveds!) may not be able to attend Mass. Bringing them the Eucharist is one of the greatest services that a parish can offer. Let's lean on Our Lady in prayer, and on Jesus in the Eucharist!

Caregivers are heroes, and their needy beloveds are much loved by God. Thank YOU for considering sharing your journey with others and spreading devotion to Our Lady of Sorrows!

Questions for Reflection and Discussion

Chapter One: The Prophecy of Simeon

Was there a moment of diagnosis that changed everything for you? Or was it a slower revelation?

How do you relate to Our Lady's slow discovery of the implications of Simeon's prophecy?

How do you feel about accepting difficult circumstances if they are the means to salvation?

Do you feel confident that God will use this time for good and not as a means of punishment?

What strikes you most about Mary that you hadn't considered before?

Chapter Two: The Flight into Egypt

What threat do you long to "flee"?

How have you experienced the gift of faith/trust during this time? How do you find strength when you don't feel that gift so strongly?

Do you feel "at home" in your role as a caregiver, or do you feel as in a foreign land?

Have you found emotional, practical, or spiritual support from another person in your life while you care for your needy beloved?

Do you feel that your hope/peace rests on rock or on "sandy ground"? How does caregiving influence your hope/peace?

What strikes you about Mary's flight into Egypt that you haven't considered before?

Chapter Three: The Loss of the Child Jesus in the Temple of Jerusalem

What aspects of your life or of your needy beloved's life feel "lost" to you?

How do you imagine Mary and Joseph felt when they were searching for Jesus? What gave them the perseverance to keep looking? What gives you perseverance?

What helps you avoid despairing about "worst case scenarios"?

How do you feel about the end of this story, when Mary and Joseph find Jesus in the temple? How does his response strike you?

Do you feel that you and your needy beloved are where you are meant to be? What emotions do you feel in attempting to reconcile this possibility?

Chapter Four: The Meeting of Mary with Jesus on His Way to Calvary

Do you find that your presence is a consolation to your needy beloved? Does someone or something else offer them comfort during this time?

What do you think of the assertion that love and sorrow are intricately bound together? Is this something you experience?

What "stars" are you able to see in the midst of this trial? What gives you hope in the coming dawn?

How do you think Mary felt as she saw Jesus on the way to Golgotha? Do you feel that you have something in common with her in that?

How do you think Jesus felt when he saw Mary? How about when he saw Simon of Cyrene helping him? Which gives you more comfort for his sake?

Chapter Five: The Death of Jesus

In what way do you experience Jesus' "thirst" as you tend to your needy beloved? For what do you "thirst"?

Do you feel that you belong to Our Lady? Do you desire to? Have you entrusted her with the care of your loved one? If not, what holds you back?

How has Mary shown her "motherliness" to you? Do you feel

that you have taken her into your heart as John took Mary into his home?

Do you relate to Saint Dismas or to the other crucified robber? Do you look upon your own temptation to snark and despair with the compassion of Christ?

What do you think Mary felt about the criminals executed next to her Son?

Chapter Six: The Piercing of the Side of Jesus and His Descent from the Cross

How do you think Mary felt when Jesus was taken down from the cross? How do you imagine the disciples around her reacted to her suffering?

What feelings and questions does this sorrow bring up for you in your life?

Which Sorrow of Mary's did you first relate to in your life?

Do you feel comfortable "keeping silence" in prayer with Mary?

How do you feel about the challenges you and your needy beloved face now? Can you begin to see these sufferings as gifts from God, or might that still be a work in progress?

Chapter Seven: The Burial of the Body of Jesus

To what extent are you able to combat the "cold calculations" that may tempt your heart?

Where have you seen God's mercy at work in your day-to-day life as a caregiver?

What is your reaction to Jesus' question, "Did you not know I would be in my Father's house?" How does his question relate to your daily experience?

Do you believe that all is as it is meant to be? What do you ask most from God?

How to Pray the Seven Sorrows of Mary Devotion (Made Easy)

P ray seven Hail Marys, meditating on one of Mary's sorrows during each prayer. It looks like this:

First Hail Mary — The Prophecy of Simeon
Second Hail Mary — The Flight into Egypt
Third Hail Mary — The Loss of the
   Child Jesus in the Temple of Jerusalem
Fourth Hail Mary — The Meeting of Mary with

Jesus on His Way to Calvary
Fifth Hail Mary — The Death of Jesus
Sixth Hail Mary — The Piercing of the Side of Jesus
  and His Descent from the Cross
Seventh Hail Mary — The Burial of the Body of Jesus

How to Pray the Little Rosary of the Seven Sorrows of Mary

(TRADITIONALLY CALLED "THE SEVEN DOLORS")

The "Little Rosary" of the Seven Sorrows of Mary includes the following prayers, as indicated by St. Alphonsus Liguori in *The Glories of Mary*. Several modern versions are available online as well. If you have access to one, you can pray this prayer using a seven sorrows rosary. The seven sorrows rosary consists of seven sets of seven beads to help you meditate on Mary's sorrows.

The Sign of the Cross
In the name of the Father, and the Son, and the Holy Spirit. Amen.

The Our Father
Our Father, Who art in heaven, hallowed be Thy name; Thy kingdom come; Thy will be done on earth as it is in heaven. Give us this day our daily bread; and forgive us our trespasses as we forgive those who trespass against us; and lead us not into temptation, but deliver us from evil.

The Hail Mary
Hail Mary, Full of Grace, The Lord is with thee. Blessed art thou among women, and blessed is the fruit of thy womb, Jesus. Holy Mary, Mother of God, pray for us sinners now, and at the hour of our death. Amen.

The Glory Be
Glory be to the Father and to the Son, and to the Holy Spirit. As it was in the beginning is now and ever shall be, world without end. Amen.

My Mother

My mother, enable my heart to share thy sorrow for the death of thy Son.

First Dolor. I pity thee, oh my afflicted mother, on account of the first sword of sorrow that pierced thee, when in the temple, by the prophecy of St. Simeon, all the cruel sufferings that men would inflict on thy beloved Jesus were represented to thee, which thou hadst already learned from the holy Scriptures, even to his death before thy eyes upon the infamous wood of the cross, exhausted of blood and abandoned by all, and thou without the power to defend or relieve him. By that bitter memory, then, which for so many years afflicted thy heart, I pray thee, oh my queen, to obtain for me the grace that always in life and in death I may keep impressed upon my heart the passion of Jesus and thy sorrows.

Our Father, Hail Mary, Glory Be, My Mother, as above.

Pray seven Hail Marys, one on each bead
of the Seven Sorrows chaplet.

Second Dolor. I pity thee, oh my afflicted mother, on account of the second sword that pierced thee when thou didst behold thy innocent Son, so soon after his birth, threatened with death by those very men for whom he had come into the world; so that thou wast obliged to flee with him by night secretly into Egypt. By the many hardships, then, that thou, a delicate young virgin, in company with thy exiled infant, didst endure in the long and wearisome journey through rough and desert countries, and in thy sojourn in Egypt, where, being unknown and a stranger, thou didst live all those years poor and despised, I pray thee oh my beloved Lady, to obtain for me the grace to suffer with patience, in thy company till death, the trials of this miserable life, that I may be able in the next to be preserved from the eternal sufferings of hell deserved by me.

Our Father, Hail Mary, Glory Be, My Mother, as above.

*Pray seven Hail Marys, one on each bead
of the Seven Sorrows chaplet.*

Third Dolor. I pity thee, oh my afflicted mother, on account of the third sword that pierced thy heart at the loss of thy dear Son, Jesus, who remained absent from thee in Jerusalem for three days, when not seeing thy beloved one by thy side, and not knowing the cause of his absence, I conceive, my loving queen, how in these nights thou didst not repose, and didst naught but sigh for him who was thy only good. By the sighs, then, of those three days, for thee so long and bitter, I pray thee to obtain for me the grace never to lose my God, that I may always live closely united to God, and thus united with him, depart from this world.

Our Father, Hail Mary, Glory Be, My Mother, as above.

*Pray seven Hail Marys, one on each bead
of the Seven Sorrows chaplet.*

Fourth Dolor. I pity thee, my afflicted mother, on account of the fourth sword that pierced thy heart, in seeing thy Jesus condemned to death, bound with ropes and chains, covered with blood and wounds, crowned with thorns, and falling under the weight of the heavy cross which he bore on his bleeding back when going like an innocent lamb to die for love of us. Thine eye then met his eye, and your glances were so many cruel arrows with which each wounded the loving heart of the other. By this great grief, then, I pray thee to obtain for me the grace to live wholly resigned to the will of my God, joyfully bearing my cross with Jesus to the last moment of my life.

Our Father, Hail Mary, Glory Be, My Mother, as above.

*Pray seven Hail Marys, one on each bead
of the Seven Sorrows chaplet.*

Fifth Dolor. I pity thee, oh my afflicted mother, on account of the fifth sword that pierced thy heart, when on Mount Calvary thou didst behold thy beloved Son, Jesus, dying slowly before thy eyes, amid so many insults, and in anguish, on that hard bed of the cross, without being able to give him even the least of those comforts which the greatest criminals receive at the hour of death. And I pray thee by the anguish which thou, oh my most loving mother, didst suffer together with thy dying Son, and by the tenderness thou didst feel, when, for the last time he spoke to thee from the cross, and taking leave of thee, left all of us to thee in the person of St. John, as thy children; and thou, still constant, didst behold him bow his head and expire; I pray thee to obtain for me the grace, by thy crucified love, to live and die crucified to everything in this world, in order to live only to God through my whole life, and thus to enter one day paradise, to enjoy him face to face.

Our Father, Hail Mary, Glory Be, My Mother, as above.

> *Pray seven Hail Marys, one on each bead*
> *of the Seven Sorrows chaplet.*

Sixth Dolor. I pity thee, oh my afflicted mother, on account of the sixth sword which pierced thy heart, when thou didst see the kind heart of thy Son pierced through and through after his death, a death endured for those ungrateful men, who, even after his death, were not satisfied with the tortures they had inflicted upon him. By this cruel sorrow, then, which was wholly thine, I pray thee to obtain for me the grace to abide in the heart of Jesus, who was wounded and opened for me; in that heart, I say, which is the beautiful abode of love, where all the souls who love God repose; and that living there, I will never love or think of anything but God. Most holy Virgin, thou canst do it; from thee I hope for it.

Our Father, Hail Mary, Glory Be, My Mother, as above.

Pray seven Hail Marys, one on each bead of the Seven Sorrows chaplet.

Seventh Dolor. I pity thee, my afflicted mother, on account of the seventh sword that pierced thy heart, on seeing in thy arms thy Son who had just expired, no longer fair and beautiful as thou didst once receive him in the stable of Bethlehem, but covered with blood, livid, and lacerated by wounds which exposed his very bones. My Son, thou saidst, my Son, to what has love brought thee? And when he was borne to the sepulchre, thou didst wish to accompany him thyself, and help to put him in the tomb with thy own hands; and, bidding him a last farewell, thou hast left thy loving heart buried with thy Son. By all the anguish of thy pure soul, obtain for me, oh mother of fair love, pardon for the offenses that I have committed against my God, whom I love, and of which I repent with my whole heart. Wilt thou defend me in temptations? Assist me at the hour of my death, that, being saved by the merits of Jesus and thine, I may come one day with thy aid, after this miserable exile, to sing in paradise the praises of Jesus and thine through all eternity. Amen.

Our Father, Hail Mary, Glory Be, My Mother, as above.

Pray seven Hail Marys, one on each bead
of the Seven Sorrows chaplet.

Concluding Prayers

Pray for us, O most sorrowful Virgin; That we may be worthy of the promises of Christ.

Let us Pray — O God, at whose passion, according to the
prophecy of Simeon, the sword of sorrow pierced through
the most sweet soul of the glorious virgin and mother,
Mary, grant that we, who commemorate and reverence
her dolors, may experience the blessed effect of thy passion,
who livest and reignest world without end. Amen.

About the Author

Theresa Kiser is a caregiver, Catholic speaker, and the author of multiple books for children including *Arthur the Clumsy Altar Server*, *Seven Gifts of Baptism*, and *Liturgical Colors*. Her life has been made vastly richer by the incredible and inspiring needy loved ones in her life, through the grace of God, whose "power is made perfect in weakness." Visit the author's website at theresakiser.com to download free printables, listen to the *Catholic Kidlit* podcast, and inquire about speaking engagements.